FINDING THE MYSTIC WITHIN YOU

Peggy Wilkinson, O.C.D.S.

LIVING FLAME PRESS
Hauppauge, N.Y. 11788

Cover: Robert Manning

Permission has been granted to quote from the following publications: From *The Collected Works of St. Teresa of Avila, Volume One*, translated by Kieran Kavanaugh, OCD, and Otilio Rodriguez, OCD, copyright © 1976, Washington Province of Discalced Carmelites, ICS Publications, 2131 Lincoln Road, N.E., Washington, D.C. 20002.

From *The Collected Works of St. Teresa of Avila, Volume Two*, translated by Kieran Kavanaugh, OCD, and Otilio Rodriguez, OCD, copyright © 1980, Washington Province of Discalced Carmelites, ICS Publications, 2131 Lincoln Road, N.E., Washington, D.C. 20002.

From *The Collected Works of St. John of the Cross* translated by Kieran Kavanaugh, OCD, and Otilio Rodriguez, OCD, copyright © 1979, Washington Province of Discalced Carmelites, ICS Publications, 2131 Lincoln Road, N.E., Washington, D.C. 20002.

From *Story of a Soul, The Autobiography of St. Therese of Lisieux*, translated by John Clarke, OCD, copyright © 1975, Washington Province of Discalced Carmelites, ICS Publications, 2131 Lincoln Road, N.E. Washington, D.C. 20002.

Thanks to *Teresian Charism Press* and *Spiritual Life* magazine for permission to include thoughts previously expressed in their publications.

Quotes from *The Jerusalem Bible*, copyright © 1966 by Darton, Longman & Todd, Ltd., and Doubleday & Company, Inc. Reprinted by permission of the publisher.

Second printing 1988

Published by:
Living Flame Press
325 Rabro Drive, Hauppauge, N.Y. 11788

ISBN: 0-914544-61-6

Copyright © Peggy Wilkinson, 1986

Printed in the United States of America
by Mark IV Press

Dedication

With much love to my husband, Tom, and our children: Lynn, her husband, Mansour Aminzadeh, and their daughter, Rana; Steve; Mike; Karen, her husband, Mark DiVincenzo, and their children, Melissa and Matthew; Donna, her husband, Mark Johnson, and their son, Mark Jr.; Gary; Greg; and Julie; my parents and, gratefully, to Our Lady of Mt. Carmel.

Acknowledgements

It would be impossible to express my love and gratitude to the Carmelite Friars for their kindness, inspiration and guidance through the years. Special thanks to Br. Bryan Paquette, OCD, for his help and encouragement; to Fr. Michael Griffin, OCD, who asked me to write my first article and would not take "no" for an answer; and to Fr. Anthony Haglof, OCD, who generously offered to write a foreword. Grateful thanks to all of the lay members of our Carmelite family, in particular the two Washington, D.C., communities of St. Joseph and Our Lady of Mt. Carmel, for all of the love, joy, pain, and spiritual support we have shared with each other.

With love and appreciation to my daughter, Lynn

Aminzadeh, OCDS, and my friend, Jude Langsam, OCDS, for their invaluable assistance; and my brothers Jim and Tom Dimond, and Tom's wife, Joan, who helped with editorial suggestions.

Introduction

In the late fifties, before Vatican II, when the Mass was still in Latin, and "meditation" was not yet a household word, I began to feel the need for a "something more" in my spiritual life. Unsure of what I was seeking, but confident that it was there in the deeper levels of my faith, I began looking for guidance. Most of the help I received came from books, for at the time, there were not many spiritual programs available at the parish level. (Fortunately, this has changed since Vatican II.)

Every book that was either by a Carmelite or about a Carmelite seemed to speak my language and answer the need that I was unable to put into words. During the sixties, the Discalced Carmelite Monastery in Washington, D.C., held Colloquiums. In 1965 my husband, Tom, brother, Jim Dimond, and I attended a series, and I discovered that there was a "Third Order" for lay people. Although I have been a Catholic all of my life, I did not remember ever hearing about "Third Orders." I found that the First Order consists of priests and brothers, the Second Order for nuns, and the Third Order is for those in the world, married or single, who continue their spiritual development in the spirit or charism of the parent order. Today, the Third Orders are called Secular Orders. In addition to Carmelites there are Dominican, Franciscan, Benedictine, etc.

When I found the Carmelite Secular Order it was like being led to an oasis after wandering alone in the desert for years, and I couldn't wait to attend meetings. My husband was somewhat bothered at what I was doing, thinking I was "trying to escape the humdrum (or hectic) house and family" (we have eight children) and reminding me that I did not have that much spare time for additional commitments. I could not accurately explain to him what it was I found in Carmel, but knew that for me it was my spiritual lifeblood.

Since my husband was a little wary, I thought it important not to let the path I had chosen cause any obvious change in our usual routine. I reassured him that my becoming a Carmelite would not interfere with our family life, and I would not expect everyone else to follow my spiritual path. I kept a low profile, and made my prayer life as unobtrusive as possible. I was professed on Trinity Sunday, 1967.

The basic Carmelite rule of life consists of a half-hour daily meditation and the Liturgy of the Hours. I said my office while feeding the baby her bottle. Since Tom worked shift work, he often came home as the children left for school; or the children would come in from school as he left for work. On those days my husband's dinner would be prepared in the middle of the day so that he could have his main meal before he left, and take a lunch to work. This meant that dinner had to be prepared again in the evening for the children. They were often a "little unruly" when Dad wasn't present at the table, and we can all laugh about it now, even me.

There was not too much in the way of "silence and solitude" in those days, and I rearranged my time for contemplative prayer daily according to the home schedule. (It is much better to be able to establish a regular time for contemplative prayer.) Eventually, an interior silence develops and establishes an inner grounding of peace, which is an immense help in the center of constant noise and activity, or as Tom sometimes described it, "the eye of the hurricane." That was how it sounded on rainy days, when he had worked all night and was trying to sleep, and children, their friends and pets were "just playing" in the house.

Interior silence is even better than exterior silence, for it can usually be depended upon. It is like a firm foundation upon which, over a lifetime, the waves of problems and illnesses, crises or disasters may crash but not crush, may shake but not shatter.

Our children are not only very active, but very loving, and I was able to see many spiritual truths clarified by just observing them, especially when they were unaware. I won't embarrass them by mentioning any of the cute things they used to do, but I keep records.

With meals, laundry, dental and doctor's appointments, homework assistance, etc., I did not have a great deal of free time. When the evening meal, homework, and children's baths were over, my bath was frequently the only available quiet space and time for my meditation.

As the children grew older, of course, it became much easier, and eventually I was even able to attend an occasional weekend retreat. Getting away from the routine for an extended time is not only refreshing, but spiritually enriching.

A few years later it was discovered that my mother was becoming senile, and she came to live with us. It was like having a baby again, as she could not be left alone. My husband and the children were wonderful and loving, but it was a very difficult time. As we heard about Alzheimer's disease, and saw some of its victims on television documentaries, we recognized the similar behavior. I resolved to keep Mother out of an institution as long as she could still recognize us, for she would become fearful if she did not at all times see a familiar face. Mother could still laugh and would enjoy herself with the children, and they would dance with her and include her in their games. I bought adult diapers and would have to shower and dress her. If I was not home my husband attended to her, for she was like an infant, completely unaware. After a few years, when her health worsened, we had to put Mother in a nursing home, but I was grateful that by this time she was beyond caring about where she was.

It has been a busy and active life, and I could not have made it without God's help, I am certain of that. The spiritual strength I received from my prayer relationship helped me to do things I never thought I would be able to do, not that I did them perfectly. Sometimes, it is enough just to endure. I often wondered how people could get through the difficulties of life that everyone encounters without inner support from God, even though they may have family support. Contemplative prayer and the Carmelite community were for me absolute necessities. Over the years, as my husband got to know many of the Carmelites, he understood why it was so important to me.

As I became familiar with the writings of Teresa of Avila and John of the Cross I could see that the spiritual journey they describe, each in their own way, is for everyone. I wondered why their writings were not more widespread, since it was obvious that everyone would not be drawn to a secular order.

The spirit of Carmel is love and contemplation. It is founded on the spirit of Elijah, who waited on the mountain in silence and solitude and found God, not in the earthshaking events of storm, wind and fire, but in the everyday, often overlooked or taken for granted "gentle breeze." The contemplative spirit requires not so much a change of life as a change of awareness, an interior change. It is not the outward circumstances of life that make a contemplative, but the inner intention of the soul.

The Order of Carmel is dedicated to Mary, who "kept the words of the Lord and pondered them in her heart." The first hermits on Mt. Carmel were called "the Brothers of Our Lady of Mt. Carmel." When they were driven out of the Holy Land because of wars, they settled in Europe.

St. Teresa of Jesus (Teresa of Avila) was born in Spain in 1515. In 1535 she entered the Convent of the Incarnation in Avila. At the time "some two hundred persons, including servants and nuns' relatives were living together at the Incarnation" (Introduction to Life). During medieval times, if women of the well-to-do families did not marry, they were often sent to convents, accompanied by servants, possessions, and even pets. Some had suites of rooms, and there was a great deal of visiting with relatives and friends. "The nuns were required to recite the Divine Office but not to observe enclosure" and "no time was designated . . . for mental prayer" (Ibid.).

Describing her prayer life, Teresa wrote that for about twenty years she lived more on the surface than in the depths until her "conversion experience." Inspired by God to return to the more interior, contemplative spirit of Carmel, she convinced John of the Cross to join her religious reform and was the only woman to have started an order for men. In 1970 St. Teresa of Avila was named the first woman Doctor of the Church.

Because Teresa and John wrote the first and most complete accounts of the various stages of the spiritual journey, their approach is usually called the "Carmelite way." Actually, it is more universal, for if the Apostles had described their own spiritual journeys, they would probably have had similar accounts, since they, too, were brought to divine transformation or "spiritual marriage." The basic spiritual journey is the same, but the experiences along the way will be different for each soul.

At the end of the Song of Songs in the Old Testament there is a conversation. St. John of the Cross writes that it is between the persons of the Trinity. "What shall we do for Our 'sister' on the day she is betrothed?" They are speaking of the soul. Each soul is the "sister" or "essence" of God, of His very "Be"-ing. Each soul comes forth from God and is meant to return to God as a bride after it is spiritually prepared.

This spiritual preparation is the basis of the spiritual journey, and contemplative prayer is an essential part of the soul's development. We are all mystics, lovers and contemplatives. Love and contemplation are the language and activity of heaven; and earth is the soul's apprenticeship for heaven. Contemplative prayer helps to develop an awareness of who we are as children of God, why we are here, and the divine destiny to which we are called.

Teresa of Avila considered prayer more as a "relationship" than "recitation," and described it as a "friendship with the Lord that grows into love." Since friendship and love are intrinsic to human nature, Teresa believed that contemplative prayer was possible for everyone willing to make the necessary preparations.

Contemplative prayer awakens inner vision, the "eyes of the soul," and can be the beginning of a "born-again" or conversion experience. Inner awareness enables the soul to see the world in a new way — the way that God sees it. As the unmistakable presence of the Indwelling God becomes clearer, prayerful souls recognize the divine in the eyes of all of their brothers and sisters, and "see" (experience) God always at work in the world beneath ordinary surface appearances.

In this Age of the Laity the Carmelite teachings are particularly relevant, especially for the current young generation. Today's young adults are the first generation to be brought up in a television age. As babies they were absorbing images and pictures every day, long before they could understand words. Pictures are irrefutable; they can touch inner depths and call forth responses. From infancy this generation has been interiorly prepared like fertile ground, open and receptive, but for many of them there was no forthcoming spiritual seed. Their conditioning has developed a singular capacity for the Divine, and only a personal, in-depth relationship with God, a Divine Intimacy, will satisfy their spiritual hunger.

God comes to each soul as it is and we, as brothers and

sisters of the same family, can love, respect, affirm, and encourage each other in our spiritual efforts, united in the same goal — if not in the same approach. As any intimate relationship is unique to the persons involved, the relationship of each soul and its Beloved is special and deeply personal. We can benefit from each other's experiences, retaining what is useful for any given stage of the soul's journey and discarding what does not relate to us. To this end I offer material which I have used through the years in leading Carmelite spiritual formation classes for our Secular members, in giving workshops on the relationship between creativity and spirituality, in leading classes on contemplative prayer in parishes, and which I have found helpful in guiding my children.

Foreword

As children we put together a working model of life, of the world as it comes to us through outside impulses and impressions. We can't function humanly without some notions of what life is, how it works, where it's going. Our minds are like jigsaw puzzles, put together from our experiences and reflections, piece by piece, day by day, over the years. Another analogy of the mind is the computer, programmed for action by training, education, "input." Computers can be reprogrammed by further input, of course, just as our working-picture or model can and ordinarily will be modified by further experience and reflection. In fact, since the mind works in coordination with a living and experiencing center, or self, in a changing world, a fundamental criterion of its health is flexibility, or capacity for change. "To live is to change," wrote Cardinal Newman, "to live well is to have changed often."

Most of us have been programmed with religious images, concepts and notions which have always been part of humankind's need to get in touch with ultimate whats, whys and wheres. As creatures of mind and imagination we can hardly imagine religion without these. The more they have been part of our training-input, other things being equal, the more seriously we take them. Little characters that we are in an uncertain world, we can't do without a sense of security, belonging, connection to something bigger. Religion gives us this. If we are not given traditional religious input, or if experience leads us to outgrow or reject notions we consider childish or superstitious, we must find connection in other ways. In his *The Art of Loving,* Erich Fromm analyzes the innumerable ways, constructive and destructive, by which people attempt to transcend the experience of separateness. According to its derivation, the word "religion" means "connect back" — to a source or meaning which gives life purpose and direction. In this basic sense most people have religion, even if they reject the term. Cut off and alone, psychologically as physically, I wither and die.

Because the religious instinct is basic and religious beliefs or dogmas not directly provable, the way is left open for numberless revelations, words, teachings, institutions, authorities, commandments, practices, images and devotions. This multifarious possibility makes religion a touchy subject in social intercourse. We learn to keep it politely in the background as we discourse about matters of more immediate concern. A philosopher said that truth is one but religion is thousands, since in the popular mind each revelation, word, etc., becomes an enclosed absolute, the firmer to grasp control of good things to be. This manipulative attitude is a necessary and unconscious element of childhood literalism, which helps me to stand and get my bearings in an otherwise unpredictable environment. The first pieces of the jigsaw puzzle come together in crisp, simple patterns. Of course there are variations, depending on many factors such as heredity, environment, background, etc. Some patterns are tighter and less vulnerable to change or rearrangement. A psychologist might attribute this to unconscious fear and insecurity, an educator to stunted environment, a philosopher to lack of understanding, a theologian to weak faith, a prophet to stiffness of neck and hardness of heart. Explanations avail little. Religion, as other fields of human concern and endeavor, has always had its settlers and its pioneers. Settlers like their pictures clear and their questions answered, even unto the number of angels that can dance on a pinhead. After defining and housebreaking God, they establish His status quo on Golden Tablets, and woe to you who doubt, deviate or question! Pioneers, some of whom may be former bored settlers, are less comfortable with a God cut down to size. They have a sense, refined by attention, that the laws, notions and devotions which superabound in religion are not after all God or reality, but only the results of finite human attempts to order, embrace or understand such. As St. John of the Cross, oft-quoted in this book, said, "God is beyond the most exalted thought we can have of Him." As the religious instinct opens the way to endless religions, the pioneer instinct opens the way to endless iconoclasm.

Humankind is not to be divided into exclusive types. We are all brainwashers and mystics, settlers and pioneers, corresponding to our basic needs for security and openness. Growth consists in balancing both in healthy tension. Theologian Karl Rahner emphasizes the importance, for Christians, of respecting tradition as the embodiment of the accumulated reflection and wisdom of the ages, yet in a later work, reflects that total humanity reaches beyond the bounds of tradition, in openness to everything and anything. This means that no religion as "enclosed garden" can be final truth as such and in itself. Religion is not for neatly separating truth from error and bludgeoning into conformity. Rather is it sensitization to Spirit, the Spirit of freedom, opportunity, and the desire to answer all my buried questions in order to be open to my deepest truth.

Pioneers have sometimes been called mystics, and herewith we approach the title of our book at hand. The social scientist Charles Fourier built much of his personality theory around what he called the "cabalist" passion, a passion for the deep and mysterious. Secrets, trips to the moon, haunted houses, faraway places, fairy tales, myths, sorcerers, wind, stars, distant isles and other things elusive, once-upon-a-time and yet-to-be arouse most people who have not slipped into practical catatonia. The arousal is a symptom of what Rahner called "openness to the infinite." Writers in the human sciences today speak more commonly of the virtues of imagination as antidote to the dullness and manipulations of ordinary life. My routines can become ruts wherein my images die and I become weighed down with the heavy side of life, without possibilities. A healthy imagination keeps me "footloose and fancy free," open to everything and anything.

But imagination can accomplish just as much for ill. Religious imagination, especially, is a fertile breeding ground of hardened fantasies and foolish ideas which make big chapters in the history of religions. Healthy imagination doesn't disconnect me from the here now, but enables me to fashion and relate to a deepening self in expansive and creative ways. Perverted imagination floats me beyond the limitations of ordinary life and locks me into castles and other airy subtleties the religious imagination is heir to. We'd all like to stop the real world and get off occasionally, but this is one way of defining craziness, as well as phoniness. And while the dividing line between sane and crazy, genuine and phony, is not always clear, common opinion has held that phony mystics outnumber real ones. This is one good reason why mystics have had a suspicious grapevine. The true mystic is simply the inner free and deepest self of each of us, in process via imagination, but emerging through the boundaries, bumps and illusions of the world we live in, the world of "common sense." This mystic knows that much of what is called "common sense" is neither common (beyond the backyard or village) nor sensible (in a changing universe in the long run), but each must discover that for herself or himself. As a Zen Master said, "The Buddha's enlightenment solved his problems; now solve yours."

For all its symbolism of power, conquest, romance, scaling the heights and plumbing the depths, the journey of growth and enlightenment is a journey within, to the core of self. Even these notions are misleading insofar as they may suggest withdrawal or escape. Genuine spirituality, or mysticism, is less concerned with the wingy mysteries of divinity than with understanding the complicated and interweaving strands of human life in the here now. This understanding is the only way to approach divinity, transcendence, mysticism, without superstition: "Let those others wear themselves out in Utopia and dream conduct which follows distant images, fruit of their invention. For the sole true invention is to decipher the present under its incoherent aspects and its contradictory language. You do not have to foresee the future but to allow it" (*Wisdom of the Saints*, Antoine de Saint-Exupery).

A more functional term than "mysticism," which Peggy Wilkinson uses and explains well in her text is "contemplation." For our present purposes, contemplation is the cutting edge of future possibilities via attention to "What's going on here?" It relates me with the working basis of my existence, my "jigsaw puzzle" state of mind, cutting through my ego patterns and fixations, the defense mechanisms by which I maintain my illusory power and control. It is a challenge to let go of little old securities, which no longer secure in a changing world, to find equilibrium in a changing universe. Sometimes it makes me feel giddy, or void, or question who I really am. Sometimes it hurts. My common sense cracks, my working model isn't working. The clay in the potter's hand cries "ouch," not knowing what the potter is up to. Only later can it be seen that pressure forms and stretches and is the stuff of growth. The process could be described in these other words: "If we want to bore to the depth of God we must take a risk. We risk something that is part of ourselves, that is the difficulty. We assume that we are deep and that the deeper we go the more delightful this God-journey becomes. . . . But it's not that simple . . . the way looks very much like the stories of the quest of the Holy Grail. There are all sorts of monsters to be met with. These monsters are not devils, not other people, just ourselves" (*Beginning to Pray*, Anthony Bloom).

Journeys without guides or guidebooks usually waste time and energy and often end up nowhere. The great, time-tested Christian guide, St. Teresa of Avila, much of whose wisdom is distilled in this book, said that her journey could have been swifter and easier with the right guidance at the right time. It's easy to imagine what could have been, and to an extent we all must learn from our mistakes, miscalculations and oversimplified schemas. God's plan for our spiritual life, said the religious psychologist Paul Tournier, is revealed by the continuous correction of our deviations. Still, much unnecessary suffering comes from our ignorance. Guides who have shared with others at different stages of their life journey (including counsellors, analysts, therapists, spiritual directors, e.g.) recall people who felt stuck, awful, depressed, phony, anxious, fearful, doubtful, "like I'm losing my mind," with no notion of "what's going on here?" We suffer much from what we don't know (if also from what we are reluctant to know) about ourselves as we relate to others and the Life out of which we come. It was for this reason that St. Teresa and St. John of the Cross, the great Carmelite mystics, shared their knowledge and experience on the spiritual path in long writings which have become Christian classics.

Peggy Wilkinson has been nourished by these writings and the Secular Carmelite Order way of life for a quarter-century. As mother of a large family she has had much contact with, and belief in, young people, whom she thinks of as hungering for something and eager to learn, even if many are "unknowing" and floundering in confusion. For many years she has been concerned to give these people, and others who cross her path, roots and guidance, some sense of value and direction in a helter-skelter society. In a recent letter she wrote: "God seems to be 'surfacing' from the deepest center of many lives. Unless they know the basics it compounds the pain. Possibly the sudden increase in youthful suicides is due to a lack of knowledge of the spiritual journey. What I see leads me to believe this." As spiritual counsellor, Peggy has often experienced how a few "basics" — the right words in the right situation — have turned things in a more constructive direction. One person known to me, whose outward circumstances were normal, experienced a darkness within and, as often happens, thought something was wrong with her mind. Referred to Peggy as she was about to see a psychiatrist, she was greatly relieved by the sharing of some of the material in this book. Of course, more basic to the "healing" or growth process than any words, new models, or techniques is understanding presence, a living teacher or experienced guide. Because the word is not the thing, simple words, images or models miss my deepest need, especially in confusion or depression: someone who understands *me*, as I am in my particularity now. This understanding is something we all need, more at some times than others. As Peggy reminds us, the basic spiritual journey is the same, but the stages of the way and experiences along the way are not the same for any two people.

But "living understanding" is rarer and, ordinarily today, more expensive than books, which at times can be very helpful sources of understanding. The material in this book has proved to be such for people of various backgrounds. St. Teresa and St. John of the Cross necessarily wrote about the Way in the language of their own times and traditions, but the Way they wrote about is universal. Besides her experience in the Carmelite tradition, Peggy Wilkinson has taught contemplative meditation in ecumenical settings and, as the book brings out, is familiar with modern spiritual writings and other schemas of growth. This book came together from material she has used in Carmelite formation classes, meditation groups, workshops and talks. It is substantially grounded in Scripture and the deepest Christian teaching on contemplative growth. For those who do not have time or inclination for long readings and study, it is a handbook of spirituality not easily found today. It provides a corrective for the many perversions of the religious instinct and other wrongheaded religious notions, a safeguard of personal freedom and spiritual growth.

Rev. Anthony Haglof, OCD

Table of Contents

1

Beginning the Practice of Contemplative Prayer

The Invitation of Jesus

"Come to Me all who labor and are heavy burdened and I will give you 'rest' for your souls [contemplation]" (Matthew 11:28). This invitation to a close personal relationship with Jesus is addressed to everyone, not just to a "spiritual elite." "Let the little ones come to Me" (Matthew 19:14). It is not the outward circumstances of life that make a contemplative, but the inner intention of the soul. The soul that acquires the habit of contemplative prayer enters into a friendship with the Lord which, over the years, deepens into mutual love.

For beginners in contemplative prayer the most important thing to remember is PRAY! and do not be overly concerned about "method." In contemplation the key word is not technique but attitude. Each soul establishes its own unique relationship with its own Indwelling God. There is a spiritual maxim, "Pray as you can, not as you ought." As the soul turns humbly to God, willing to be led, the beginnings of change are set in motion. It is never too late for a new beginning. "The promise of reaching the place of 'rest' He had for them still holds good, and NONE of you must think that He has come too late for it" (Hebrews 4:1).

Some people refer to this "new beginning" as a "born-again" or "conversion" experience. In the New Testament

John the Baptist referred to it as "metanoia." "Metanoia" has often been translated as "repentance," but more accurately means a "turning around," a change of attitude or inner direction, a complete turning of the heart, soul and mind to God. This "turning around" is dramatically portrayed in the account of St. Paul's experiential encounter with the risen Christ on the road to Damascus. For most people it starts in a much more ordinary way. The usual conversion experience can begin with a joyful occasion: falling in love; the birth of a child; an intense awareness of the presence of God in the Eucharist, in the self or another person; or in the beauty of nature. It can also start in a painful way such as the loss of a loved one, a serious illness or accident, any event powerful enough to affectively touch the latent potential of the soul and awaken its perception.

The soul's faculties can be gently awakened through the practice of contemplative prayer. To experience in prayer the unmistakable presence of the Indwelling God not only activates inner vision, but stirs an in-depth response. This inner commitment may not actually be formed in words, but intuitively sensed and expressed with the whole self, a movement of the heart which initiates the intention and desire to be God-motivated in every area of our lives. True spiritual commitment means that our inner relationship with God permeates and influences every aspect of our daily routine.

This attitude before God is all-important for ongoing spiritual development. It forms the nature of our response to the invitation of the Lord. "Behold I stand at the door and knock" (Revelation 3:20). Our response is necessary to open the "inner door" of our will and allow the rays of divine love to penetrate, to allow the dawning of divine wisdom. If our bodies give us a warning signal we usually attend to it in short order. When the Lord signals us from within, we should give Him our undivided attention.

In its humble attitude of prayer, the contemplative soul

wordlessly expresses the heartfelt cry: "Lord, that I may see" (Matthew 20:33). As Jesus explained to Nicodemus (John 3:1) we cannot physically be "born again," but in spiritual re-birth the eyes of the soul are opened and gradually begin to "see" like a newborn infant. "Unless a man is born from above he cannot 'see' the Kingdom of God" (John 3:1). The world of the spirit can only be "seen" with the "eyes of the soul."

Jesus made frequent references to this lack of inner comprehension in His preaching: "You will listen and listen again, but not understand, see and see again, but not perceive" (Matthew 13:14). "If you in your turn had only understood on this day the message of peace! But, alas, it is hidden from your eyes! . . . You did not recognize your opportunity when God offered it" (Luke 19:42, 44).

In contemplative prayer as we absorb Love (God), we absorb ALL of the attributes of God (divine wisdom, gentleness, mercy, forgiveness, compassion, etc.), and our understanding constantly increases as these divine qualities gradually become the soul's qualities also. The inspired words of Scripture contain a wealth of hidden meanings, and discernment depends upon inner vision. All of the spiritual books that we read, whether for guidance or inspiration, will be more comprehensible through this heightened interior perception. "The Light shines in the darkness, and the darkness grasped it not" (John 1:5). Contemplative prayer is an essential part of the soul's progress from darkness (imperfect human knowledge) to light (Divine Wisdom).

Seeing is contingent upon light. "I, the Light, have come into the world, so that whoever believes in Me need not stay in the dark anymore" (John 12:46). "See to it then that the light inside you is not darkness" (Luke 11:35). Our earthly lives provide us with the time and opportunities for transcending the merely natural inner darkness, or non-comprehension, and becoming "children of light."

To become a spiritual child is the next step in the "born-again" experience. When Jesus was making a particularly significant statement, He preceded it with, "I tell you solemnly," to emphasize its importance to His followers. "I tell you solemnly, unless you change and become like little children you will never enter the Kingdom of Heaven" (Matthew 18:3). "The mysteries of the Kingdom of God are revealed to you" when you "welcome the Kingdom of God like a little child" (Luke 8:9; 18:17). To the "little ones" ready to accept the Kingdom like children, Jesus addressed His message. The little ones were the "anawim," the lowly, the poor of God, those who did not rate in the eyes of the world. Aware of their need, they were like the thirsty earth soaking up the rain and absorbed into themselves the example and teachings of Jesus. Acceptance in trust, without fully understanding, is faith in action and implies love, the solid foundation and unifying principle of a spiritual relationship. When a couple decide to marry they not only profess their love in words but in a lifetime commitment. Trust is self-evident, for they have no guarantee of what the future may hold.

It takes childlike simplicity and humility to recognize and accept our littleness, our weakness, and inability to bring about our own spiritual growth and perfection. The trusting child depends entirely upon the parents for its love, care, guidance, food, and protection. By the giving and receiving of love and care, a "bond" is formed and, in the process, the child gradually becomes "like" the parents, "equals" on an adult level. A similar process takes place in the spiritual dimension between God and the soul.

"Religion: Re (again) + ligare (to bind), to bind again or bind strongly. 'Religion' means a bond between God and human beings." It is a bond of love forged in the spirit. Without this inner relationship, outer rituals and regulations are empty and meaningless, merely a matter of going through the motions, like a marriage arranged for business purposes or reasons of state.

"They will keep up the outward appearance of religion

but will have rejected the inner power of it" (2 Timothy 3:5). "This people honours Me only with lip-service, while their hearts are far from Me. The worship they offer Me is worthless" (Matthew 15:8). Jesus taught that the Father desires "worship in spirit and truth," which pre-supposes a heart-to-heart relationship.

Children must first receive love before they are able to love in return. Psychologists state that children who are denied love in the early years do not develop as they should and, in extreme cases, have even died from lack of love. A comparable principle holds true in the spiritual development of the soul. Without the receiving and returning of divine love the soul languishes.

Many times when a child seems troublesome it is because, for some reason, he or she feels unloved or lonely, not able to feel good about himself or herself, and a touch of love or a hug melts his or her defenses, overcoming that sense of spiritual isolation and human separateness to which all human beings are subjected. Even little children have the instinct that we all need each other and, in their spiritual simplicity, have a vivid sense of the healing power of love that takes place on the spiritual level, even though they would not be able to put it into words. When the soul, like the little child, feels troubled, it is a great help to come into the presence of God and "rest" in that Divine embrace. I have a very dear friend who is a Brother in the Discalced Carmelite Monastery. Through the years we have had many a telephone conversation, usually discussing or debating spiritual issues. When one or the other of us was "down," we would send each other "hugs" over the phone. If nothing else, it would start us laughing which helps to keep everything in perspective, while it aids the spiritual healing process.

"Laughter is a sudden, explosive release of happy energy, a rippling cry of joy only humans utter and understand, it dissolves hate, heals the sick, and binds humanity together in a common fellowship only humans can

27

join. . . . Comedy is fulfillment, accomplishment, overcoming. It is victory over odds, a triumph of good over evil. Tragedy is frustration, failure, despair. The evil in man prevails; there is mourning.

"Comedy is good news. . . . The Gospels are comedies: a triumph of spirit over matter. The Resurrection is the happiest of all endings: man's triumph over death. The Mass is a 'celebration' of that event. Priests and parishioners 'celebrate' a Mass. It is a divine comedy.

"In social terms, comedy is a complete surrender of one's defenses. If you don't like a certain person your defenses are up. No laughs. . . . But you laugh easily among friends, you love them, you let down your defenses. You laugh easily among the innocent — babies for instance. Five of the greatest humorists that made the world ring with laughter were priests: Rabelais, Sterne, Scarron, Swift, and Sidney Smith. . . . Man is the only animal that can laugh and has a soul" *(The Name Above the Title,* Frank Capra).

Children have the natural ability to live completely in the present moment, and are usually not overly concerned about tomorrow. In our earthly existence, of course, as mature, responsible adults we have to make plans to support ourselves and our families. But in the spiritual realm, the Lord reveals His plans for us one day at a time. Just as we cannot store up enough food in our bodies to last a year, or even a month, God has designed a similar process for spiritual development. "Give us this day, our daily bread" includes nourishment for the soul as well as the body.

God invites us to come to Him daily, a regular time for recommitting our wills, giving Him our undivided attention, and growing in our realization of our need of, and our complete dependence upon Him as the source of the soul's development. This realization encourages growth not only in divine love, but in faith, gratitude and humility. He reveals His way one step at a time because He knows the tendencies to pride of the human beings He created. With a long-range plan or schedule, we might say, "We can take it from here; we won't be needing You anymore." More importantly, God instills only what the soul is capable of receiving.

The Israelites wandering in the desert were instructed by God to gather no more than one day's supply of manna at a time. Human beings, being "more practical," would gather a week's supply at a time, or even freeze-dry enough for a year. But "God's ways are not man's ways," and Jesus re-echoes the command in "Give us this day our daily bread." We must remember at all times who we are as creatures in relation to our Creator, experiencing our need, and then responding with our faithful presence and attentive listening.

"A child of God listens to the words of God" (John 8:47). The development of the soul requires a childlike turning toward God on a regular basis. To "learn from God" and "become like" another, it is necessary to "be with" the other. It takes time for growth and change. Spiritual development is far more than a matter of learning and storing information; it is a progressive "becoming." Just as "we are what we eat," the soul "becomes" what it absorbs from God. Keeping this principle in mind helps the soul to remain faithful to its regular time of contemplative prayer. Just as we do not feel ourselves growing as we move from infancy to childhood, we will not always be immediately conscious of a spiritual change in the soul. Remaining faithful to prayer without discerning an immediate benefit calls forth a greater faith response and strengthens hope and love. It is only through spiritual hindsight and a gradual heightened contemplative awareness that the soul is able to recognize that it is not what it once used to be.

The strengthening of the virtues, especially love, is a necessary part of the soul's development. Often people mistakenly give up the habit of contemplative prayer because they "do not get anything out of it." Real love is giving, not getting. We give God the gift of our time daily, unconditionally, as our reflection of His love for us. If divine love is growing in the soul this attitude of self-lessness will be present. Being faithful to the time of prayer is all that is required of us; the rest is up to God.

"I tell you solemnly, this poor widow has put more in than all who have contributed to the treasury; for they have all put in money they had over, but she, from the little she had, has put in everything she possessed, all she had to live on" (Mark 12:43).

We are all busy and our time is precious. Something valuable to us is the only thing worth offering to God, so we should give time from "the little that we have to live on." It is a case of putting first things first, "seek first the Kingdom of God." We should not try to fit God into our spare time like a hobby, but must rearrange our priorities.

In silent, expectant waiting, we try to discern God's will for us, not try to convince Him of ours, since the land of the spirit is not always the way that we might imagine it. As the soul develops and changes, its needs will vary, and God alone knows the state of the soul and its requirements at each stage. The spiritual world is God's territory. It is vast and unknown, and we must trust completely in our Guide and His provisions. Childlike love, trust and utter dependence upon God are conditions for "entering" (participating in) the Kingdom.

The Saints were able to highlight points of the Gospel, thereby bringing them into focus for the rest of us. A Carmelite nun, St. Therese, the "Little Flower," emphasized the "little way of spiritual childhood." "I understand so well that it is only love which makes us acceptable to God. . . . Jesus deigned to show me the road that leads to this Divine Furnace, and this road is the surrender of the little child who sleeps without fear in its Father's arms. . . . Jesus does not demand great actions from us but simply surrender and gratitude" (Story of a Soul, Fr. John Clarke, OCD, p. 188). Centuries before her the foundress of the Discalced Carmelite Order, St. Teresa of Avila, wrote in her *Interior Castle*, "The Lord doesn't look so much at the greatness of our works as at the love with which they are done" (VII: 4, 15).

We should not hold ourselves distant from God through some false humility over mere human weakness and failures. It is our weakness that draws God to us, just as a helpless infant draws the attention of all of the adults around him. A parent runs to the child most in need. To feel that one is "unworthy" to seek a closer relationship with God would be like saying one is too sick to see a doctor. Cooperating with God's love as it does its healing work is all that is required of us. " 'My grace is enough for you: My power is at its best in weakness.' So I shall be very happy to make my weaknesses my special boast so that the power of Christ may stay over me . . . for it is when I am weak that I am strong" (2 Corinthians 12:9). As we humbly accept our spiritual powerlessness, God progressively infuses His own divine strength.

Humble obedience and cooperation are essential for spiritual progress. "Obedience" is taken from the Latin "ob + audire — to hear completely." Spiritual writers have said that obedience is the respect that love pays to authority, and God is THE Authority ("supremacy, dominion") over His creatures.

St. Teresa of Avila tells us, "Humility is truth." Humility helps us to become aware of the vast difference between the Creator and the created while, at the same time, acknowledging with certainty that HE LOVES US ANYWAY.

Let us keep in mind that human qualities such as being in charge, saving time, and achieving results may be assets in the business world, but these traits must be temporarily set aside as we come before God like trusting children, letting the spiritual child in each of us lead us to the Father. "The calf and lion cub feed together, and a little child shall lead them" (Isaiah 11:6).

The Command of Jesus

"Jesus said, 'You must love the Lord your God with all your heart, with all your soul, with all your mind, and with all your strength. This is the greatest and the first commandment. The second resembles it: you must love your neighbor as yourself' " (Matthew 22:37).

All prayer can lead to contemplative prayer, for if our minds and hearts were not on God we would not really be praying.

Love of God comes before love of neighbor, is expressed and grows stronger in practicing love of neighbor, and empowers and re-energizes the soul for ongoing service. Turning to God first in a listening attitude ensures that we have an habitual reverence for the presence of God in others, regardless of their worldly status. This inner awareness of the Indwelling Presence helps us to "see" God always at work in the world beneath ordinary surface appearances. It is of great spiritual benefit to the soul to keep in mind the presence of the divine within the human. It reduces the risk of trying to enforce one's own will, be overly controlling, manipulative, or self-seeking.

Love of neighbor is the other side of prayer. Love is the only thing that increases by giving it away. Flowing water does not become stagnant. The Spirit is dynamic, and the streams of Living Water are copious. As a result of our intention of allowing God's love to come through us as willing instruments, divine love, infused by God during prayerful stillness, overflows like a hidden spring into all of our day-to-day activities, whether it is in the immediate family, in a professional capacity, or as self-giving on a volunteer basis. God is living, loving, and working in us and through us, and this divine love, far surpassing human love, is how we are able to genuinely love our "neighbor." God loves the neighbor through us, thereby making whatever help and care we are able to give far more fruitful.

"As a branch cannot bear fruit all by itself, but must remain part of the vine, neither can you unless you remain in Me . . . for cut off from Me you can do nothing" (John 15:4-5).

"We will not reach perfection in the love of neighbor if that love doesn't rise from love of God as its root" (Interior Castle, St. Teresa of Avila, V:3, 9).

"It is impossible to love Christ without loving others . . . and it is impossible to love others . . . without moving nearer to Christ" (Divine Milieu, Teilhard de Chardin, p. 144).

Love of neighbor means to respond to a need, to have a care and concern; it does not necessarily require warm, affectionate feelings toward the "neighbor." This is not the meaning of "love." Some people may feel needlessly guilty about this, but it would be humanly impossible to be close friends with everyone. Even Jesus had special friends during His earthly life, although His love was non-exclusive. It is natural to have friends that one enjoys, and to meet other people with whom we may have little or nothing in common, but if these people were in need, the absence of affectionate feelings should not prevent our response as "good Samaritans." Spiritually, we are all sisters and brothers. "If one part is hurt, all parts are hurt with it" (1 Corinthians 12:26).

Through its contemplative relationship with God, the soul becomes more open and vulnerable. Love implies trust and, like David facing Goliath, it is necessary to put aside our outer shell, the armor of pride and defensiveness, and place our confidence fully in God. Love involves the risk of being hurt, but the soul cannot be open to God in prayer and closed to its brothers and sisters. "A man who does not love the brother [sister] that he can see, cannot love God Whom he has never seen" (John 5:20). As our inner vision becomes clearer, we begin to recognize divinity in the eyes of all of our brothers and sisters and, more importantly, live and act accordingly. In experiencing the reality of our own divine/human spirit, we can more fully understand and identify with the earthly life of the God-man, Jesus.

The teachings of Jesus reveal the spiritual dynamic of an inward and outward flow. The recurring theme in the process of spiritual development that Jesus used to instruct His followers was first the invitation to "Come follow Me," "Learn from Me," and "Live in Me"; and then it became the command to "Go, and teach all nations," "Love one another," and "Bear one another's burdens." Receptive souls are filled more and more with divine love during quiet time in the presence of Jesus. This "living water" then flows outward through the channels of souls as love of neighbor.

Throughout His earthly life Jesus exemplified the importance of contemplation by regularly taking time for solitary prayer even when the needy crowds surrounded Him. "Large crowds would gather to hear Him and to have their sickness cured, but He would always go off to some place where He could be alone and pray" (Luke 5:15). "In the morning, long before dawn, He got up and left the house, and went off to a lonely place and prayed there" (Mark 1:35).

Before they could be of any spiritual benefit or influence in the world, the Apostles had to first spend quiet time in the presence of Jesus. They had to be open to the infusion of Divine Love and Light before they could spread that same love and light in the world for, in the spiritual area, we can give only what we have, and what we are inside.

Not only do we "give," but we are constantly "projecting" what we are inside. In our spiritual depths we are all one, so that what we are at each moment and what we are constantly becoming necessarily affect each other. Through its ever-developing Image of Christ, the contemplative soul will project a comparable inner harmony into the daily round of activities and relationships. The desire for power, possessions, or the prejudices of the self-centered soul, multiplied by billions of individuals, is manifested as conflict in the world. Contemplative souls are not only filled with a sense of divine peace, love, and joy for themselves, but for all whose lives touch theirs and, eventually, all mankind.

Although the Apostles were uneducated and had no positions of influence in the world, they did have the child-like attitude necessary for spiritual growth and divine transformation. They were open, willing to listen, and to change if necessary. They were willing to be led, and were receptive as the Divine Light formed each of their souls in its own unique divine Image.

When Jesus took on a human nature, the Divine became enfleshed and made visible to human eyes. In His earthly life Jesus reflected to the world the Image and message of the Father. "Do you not believe that I am in the Father and the Father is in Me? The words I say to you I do not speak as from Myself: it is the Father, living in Me, Who is doing this work" (John 14:10). As Jesus by His divine nature manifested the Father, the Apostles, through their divine transformation, brought to the world the Image, the love, and the teachings of Jesus.

The more that we love, the more capacity we will have for ever greater divine love (agape), which is necessary in order to fulfill our obligation to "Love one another as I have loved you" (John 15:12). This command of Jesus sounds simple enough when we read it, but it loses something in the translation when we try to put it into practice. Agape love is not a self-centered love concerned with one's own gain, or whether or not the other person deserves our love. Agape love is unconditional and non-exclusive. "What proves that God loves us is that Christ died for us while we were still sinners" (Romans 5:7).

"If I have all the eloquence of men or angels, but speak without love [agape], I am simply a gong booming or a cymbal clashing. If I have the gift of prophecy, understanding all the mysteries there are, and knowing everything, and if I have faith in all its fullness, to move mountains, but without love, then I am nothing at all. If I give away all that I possess, piece by piece, and if I even let them take my body to burn it, but am without love, it will do me NO GOOD WHATEVER . . . there are three things that last: faith, hope and love; and the greatest of these is love" (1 Corinthians 13:1-3).

"Love [agape] has no possessiveness and is not a desire for satisfaction; it wants to satisfy the other. This love is attributed to God the Father, but as it is identical with God's nature, it is found in the Son. . . . This is the same love that the Holy Spirit gives Christians to help them to carry out the essential commandment of the Law, love of God and neighbor" (1 Corinthians 13a).

The close relationship to God in contemplative prayer is one of the primary means to growth in agape love, which is a prerequisite for loving as Jesus loved. As we encourage God's selfless love to grow and develop within us, it becomes easier to control and restrict our self-centeredness. "He must increase, I must decrease" (John 3:30).

The beginner in contemplative prayer, especially, needs a regular time of silence and solitude, time "alone with the Alone." Gradually, an interior silence develops and the world itself seems changed but, in reality, it is our attitude.

> *I love to gather flowers*
> *That I find along the highway,*
> *Discarded by some pilgrims*
> *Because their petals wilted.*
> *And I place them all before Him,*
> *For they're all I have to offer,*
> *With silent conversations*
> *In the cloister of my heart.*
>
> *And as I sit beside Him,*
> *All my troubles seem to vanish.*

I can't recall their number
Or just what it was that plagued me.
For He shares with me His riches,
Takes pity on this leper,
Touches me with mercy
In the cloister of my heart.

And it doesn't seem to matter
That my home is not a castle,
For He's used to shabby stables
And friends who are not wealthy.
Then His love begins to shame me,
For He asks so very little
In return for All He offers
In the cloister of my heart.

All the world seems strangely silent
Just as long as He is speaking.
The time no longer passes
And I can't remember breathing.
For His Presence is transforming
And the Splendor of it lingers,
Through all the lonely winters
In the cloister of my heart.

Problems and annoyances of everyday life do not seem able to reach our inner tranquility — not because the soul ceases to care, because it actually cares more — only now it is with God's care and concern, as we see through His eyes, love with His love, and have complete confidence in His wisdom even though we may not fully understand, like the little child, not yet wise, has complete trust in the parents.

This development has been compared to the depths of the ocean, which are calm and still, even though violent storms may be raging on the surface. There is also an acceptance of our limitations, and an adjustment of our idea of "perfection." Another dear friend, a Carmelite priest, said that when he was first ordained he thought he had to have an answer for every spiritual doubt, but as he grew older and wiser, he "learned to live with mystery." This seemed a beautiful acknowledgement of the omniscient God, and the humble acceptance of the position of the creature in relation to his Creator.

"Ours is a time of anxiety because we have willed it to be so. Our anxiety is not imposed on us by force from outside. We impose it on our world and upon one another from within ourselves. Sanctity in such an age means, no doubt, travelling from the area of anxiety to the area in which there is no anxiety or perhaps it may mean learning, from God, to be without anxiety in the midst of anxiety. Fundamentally, as Max Picard points out, it probably comes to this: living in a silence which so reconciles the contradictions within us that, although they remain within us, they cease to be a problem. Contradictions have always existed in the soul of man. But it is only when we prefer analysis to silence that they become a constant and insoluble problem. We are not meant to resolve all contradictions but to live with them and rise above them and see them in the light of exterior and objective values which make them trivial by comparison. Silence, then, belongs to the substance of sanctity" (*Thoughts in Solitude*, Thos. Merton, pp. 82-83).

Silence has always been the biblical symbol heralding the Presence of God. Even in the natural world silence can be eloquent. When two people first meet they may engage in a great deal of "small talk." If the friendship develops into love, it is enough just to be together in silence, intensely, acutely, and lovingly aware of each other's presence. At this stage there is no need for words because of a love so profound that it is beyond words. St. John of the Cross wrote, "Silence is the language of love." Contemplative prayer provides a space of silence in our depths for the soul's tranquil "resting" in God. This interior silence gradually becomes an habitual state of being, the soul's apprenticeship for heaven.

In heaven we will all be contemplatives, and our heavenly life has its beginnings on earth. Earthly life is our preparation time for "Life is the childhood of our eternity" (Goethe). From the beginning of our existence we have the potential within ourselves and need only time in which to develop awareness of who we are as children of God, and the sublime destiny to which we are called.

Contemplation is an integral part of action; they are not contradictory. All lives, to be whole, need both. Contemplation animates and sustains action, consecrating our most insignificant activities. It could be described as Mary's heart in Martha's body — Mary's heart remaining at the feet of Jesus in the contemplative loving gaze, while Martha goes about the daily routine. Human nature has a tendency to separate and compartmentalize everything, but the divine and the human aspects of our humanity cannot be separated. It is precisely through our humanity that we are meant to develop into our "God-likeness."

"We are constantly forgetting that the supernatural is a ferment, a soul, and not a complete and finished organism. Its role is to transform 'nature'; but it cannot do so apart from the matter which nature provides it with" (Divine Milieu, Teilhard de Chardin, p. 152).

"The glory of God is man fully alive" (St. Ireneaus).

"The more we become whole, the more we become holy" (Fr. Wm. McNamara, OCD).

Becoming a "contemplative" in the world is not a negative withdrawing from the world, or a self-centered occupation aimed solely at self-improvement. It is a positive step, a potential growth experience, just as seeking an education would be, or developing our talents. It is our responsibility to develop our fullest potential in every facet of our humanity. By opening our souls to God and allowing Him to transform them, we will be of far more benefit to ourselves and to others.

"Let us desire and be occupied in prayer not for the sake of our enjoyment but so as to have this strength to serve" (Interior Castle, St. Teresa of Avila, VII:4, 12).

Spiritual growth and healing through contemplative

prayer are not only for our own benefit but for the world, just as individual efforts to guarantee fresh, clear air, and unpolluted water are beneficial for everyone. We are all connected in the spirit. As Jesus was a carrier and a channel for the Father's love, we, by growing in His Spirit, become "go-betweens," bridges between heaven and earth. The Spirit of Christ, multiplying in endless humanities, brings healing love to the world. Through these go-betweens as willing instruments, the glance that turned water into wine and sinners into saints will again effect cures, and there will be "a new Heaven and a new earth."

When people have been ill for some time they often become confused, and cannot think of a remedy. Others must provide treatment until they are stronger, and aware enough to help themselves. In contemplative prayer we keep the mirror of our souls turned to the "Sun of Love," not solely to bask in its rays for our own enjoyment, but to reflect the Healing Light back to a wounded world, like a divine laser beam that cauterizes, purifies, and heals the inner woundedness. God's love does not come just "to" us, but "through" us. As Fr. Edward Farrell so aptly put it in *Disciples and Other Strangers,* "Something more than myself is what I want to give you."

Through our human faults we are all a part of the world's "sickness." Into the loving presence of God each day we bring a broken world, a fractured humanity. We bring it trustingly, with the unbounded confidence of the little child who is certain that his Father can fix anything. With His glance Jesus healed the sick, the leper, sanctified the "Good Thief," and transformed Mary Magdalene. "If Thou wilt, Thou could make me whole," is the cry of the world groaning in its "dark night."

"From the beginning till now the entire creation, as we know, has been groaning in one great act of giving birth" (Romans 8:22). Before the collective act of giving spiritual birth becomes an earthly reality (parousia), the willingness of each soul to cooperate in its own personal transformation is necessary.

God's attitude toward His creatures has always been

one of divine graciousness and courtesy. As God awaited Mary's consent before the Lord came to earth in a human nature, He awaits the consent and inner commitment of souls before He works in them and through them, to reflect the fullness of the parousia through His mystical body.

In God's attitude of reverence and respect for each individual's free will and uniqueness, we find an important lesson for ourselves. Having imparted to us His very nature and free will, God does not then enforce His will upon us. His purpose requires the process of synchronizing human and divine will, and so He awaits our response in love, the effort of committing our will at every stage of the spiritual journey, before proceeding with the next step in His plan to unite the soul to Himself.

During His earthly life, Jesus displayed this same reverential attitude. In deference to the divine freedom and uniqueness of each person, Jesus always took the time to deal with each one on an individual basis. In spite of the obvious needs of the poor and sick that thronged around Him, He did not deal with the crowd as an anonymous group. In the Gospel accounts of healing and ministering, Jesus sought out one individual at a time, giving that person His complete and undivided attention, even if it meant that the rest of the people had to make the effort to seek Him out another day.

A one-to-one relationship is essential for spiritual growth, healing, and love. To us, as His followers, this attitude of Jesus says much, for we realize we are deeply loved, each soul in its own special relationship. God's love has been there from the beginning; it doesn't start at the point when the soul suddenly becomes aware of being loved. In contemplative prayer the soul is able to experience that "God has loved us so much . . . we are to love, then, because He loved us first" (1 John 4:11, 19).

In His sympathy for the frailty of human nature, which He shared, Jesus always showed mercy, forgiveness, and compassion for sinners. His criticism was not for those who were weak, but for those who were judgmental and rigid, following the "letter of the law," when "it is the spirit that gives life" (John 6:63).

Those who are humanly weak and make mistakes recognize their need to improve, and are therefore open to change. Those who adhere only to the letter of the law are too often self-satisfied with their "accomplishments." Considering themselves already holier than others, they see no need to change, and are not reachable. The Pharisees, in their scrupulous outer conformity to the law, were denounced as hypocrites, "white-washed sepulchres," interiorly dead but putting up a good front. "If your virtue goes no deeper than that of the scribes and Pharisees, you will never get into the Kingdom of Heaven" (Matthew 5:20).

Too often, people in positions of authority become inordinately fond of power, and try to use rules as a means of controlling others. Because they have made the letter of the law an end in itself rather than making an effort to change, they attempt to enforce this attitude upon the people. "Alas for you, scribes and Pharisees, you hypocrites! You who shut up the kingdom of heaven in men's faces, neither going in yourselves nor allowing others to go in who want to" (Matthew 23:13).

Throughout His earthly life Jesus exemplified the importance of surrender of human will, and the inward and outward flow of love of God, love of neighbor. He periodically renewed His human spirit in solitary communing with the Father, discerning the Father's will and obeying. Jesus did not follow His own will during His earthly life, even though He was Son by nature. "His state was divine, yet He did not cling to His equality with God but emptied Himself to assume the condition of a slave, and became as men are; and being as all men are, He was humbler yet" (Philippians 2:6).

Jesus healed the sick and fed the hungry even on the Sabbath, thereby living the original intent and purpose of the law. Jesus spoke harshly to those whose outer conformity had no influence on their inner growth in divine love, but who hardened themselves in self-centeredness and pride. "If you had understood the meaning of the words: 'What I want is mercy, not sacrifice,' you would not have condemned the blameless. For the Son of Man is master of the Sabbath" (Matthew 12:7-8).

Jesus taught, "It is the spirit that gives life," and the life-giving power of the spirit is love. Love conquers all; it supersedes the rule. Rules are meant to be like guardrails, which help to keep us from swerving off the road during the earthly phase of our journey home. Rules are not meant to be roadblocks or barricades that prevent us from moving closer to God, which they can be if following the letter of the law becomes an end in itself. This attitude puts rules in the place reserved for God alone.

When in doubt, lead with the heart for, with God, hearts are always "trump." Some people believe that following the letter of the law is safe; they give exactly what is expected of them, no more, no less, while there is a risk in leading with the heart. A person could be more vulnerable and open to pain. But being open and growing is to experience life to its fullest. Life is meant to be lived, not observed from a safe distance by spectators who avoid getting involved. The meaning of life is only realized through an ever-growing love, and real love means to give without counting the cost, giving all. Through this self-giving love the soul will more and more mirror the divine. It doesn't matter how much or how little we have to give, as long as we give ALL that we are capable of giving. Human nature is hesitant: "Master, what about us?" (Mark 10:28).

"The amount you measure out is the amount you will be given" (Matthew 7:3).

"I myself hold that the measure for being able to bear a large or small cross is love" (Way of Perfection, St. Teresa of Avila, ch. 32:7).

2

The Nature of Contemplative Prayer

"Contemplation" may have different meanings for different individuals and is therefore used to cover a wide range of prayer experiences. The word "contemplation" is based on the Latin "templum — open space for observation of the heavens, which also gives us temple." In contemplation we descend into our inner space to observe heavenly things.

In the spiritual sense, "contemplation" goes far beyond Aristotle's distinction between " 'praktikos' — practical — and 'theoretikos' — contemplative, speculative," because in the spiritual area it involves far more than mere abstract thinking. In contemplation we become open to a new dimension of existence which is actual, though invisible, and are in touch with the Absolute in a growth process meant to transcend the human and natural, a process which is the answer to humanity's longing for the divine and eternal.

Contemplative prayer has been described as "a loving gaze upon God with the eyes of the soul." It is important to remember concerning the loving gaze that we WILL it, not that we necessarily always FEEL it, for love acts and intensifies through commitment to the will. Like "contemplation," the word "love" covers a wide range of experiences and emotions on the human level. On the divine level, love is an overwhelming, unifying force, a purifying, transforming fire, which we can only receive through God's generous Self-giving. Love is not always synonymous with warm, affectionate feelings even in human love.

Although there may be exhilaration and tender feelings during the engagement and early years of marriage, in order to survive, love must sink deeper roots, into the "groundwater" of our being. As love reaches down into the vaster area of spirit it begins to exist below the sense level. In these inner depths love goes about its unifying work and, although love is always present and active, surface emotions may not always be evident. This coalescing of spirits, which is love's work, ensures a far more profound and enduring love than the merely physical, for the spiritual area is infinite and timeless.

By its extension into and activity in the spiritual dimension, love activates and nourishes the growth and completion of the intrinsic masculine/feminine attributes of the soul. For this process the answering reflection of an opposite who is entirely "other," and an echoing love from a corresponding depth is required. The love of husband and wife aiding and encouraging one another's spiritual development is one reason why marriage is considered sacred by most religions. Even without the possibility of having children, the fact that spiritual growth is gradual and progressive requires that marriage be a lifetime commitment. Spiritual and natural love, together, provide life's most beneficial environment and solid foundation, not only for husband and wife, but for children who are healthy in body, mind, and spirit.

There are no easy loves. Growth in love doesn't just happen, but requires an effort from both husband and wife. Love is kept alive and growing through constant care, attention, and consideration. After ten, twenty, or thirty years of marriage, the love of husband and wife is strengthened and richer. The friction and differences of the early years have been mostly resolved, as each partner learns to be more selfless and giving, and husband and wife become more compatible and attain a "like-mindedness."

Couples who have weathered the stormy years of marriage usually see that they have grown closer to each other, and there is a oneness of spirit that could not have been accomplished any other way. This uniting in spirit is the primary purpose of marriage, a union that is far more than physical closeness which could be merely superficial. Sexual union is meant to be an expression of love and spiritual union. Husband and wife are the earthly representation of the Trinity. The human, natural love of husband and wife, expressed in physical union which may generate a child, reflects the dynamic supernatural love and spiritual union within the Trinity, which generates a new soul.

As husband and wife grow together in ever-deepening interior union over the years, an invisible bond is formed and, even when apart, the two are one in spirit in a way that cannot be described. With that experience comes the unshakeable conviction of its reality and a profound sense of "completeness," by the fusing of formerly disparate beings. In these beings creation is restored and made whole. There is an at-one-ment ("harmony, reconciliation") as the two halves of human nature, male and female, are once more harmoniously one in spirit, as masculine and feminine exist within the Trinity. The Trinity consists of three separate, dynamic Persons, equal but different, One in love and will to such a degree that there is no desire to exert control over the Other.

"Where love rules, there is no will to power, and where power predominates, there love is lacking" (Carl Jung).

The spiritual oneness of masculine and feminine of the marriage partners helps to clarify the similar development towards wholeness within the individual soul. Each soul is meant to reach divine completeness and like-mindedness through the ever-increasing compatibility of human will with divine will, and by developing a harmonious balance of the masculine/feminine capacities within the soul itself. In order for the soul to be transformed, all of its capacities must be prepared to accurately mirror those of the divine. Souls come forth from harmony and are meant to return, having attained their own inner harmony.

The earthly process differs in that it begins with marriage and, in the spiritual journey, it ends with marriage. Fortified by the grace of the Sacrament, earthly marriage provides the means through which husband and wife become compatible and grow together as one. As human beings husband and wife start out as equals; God and the soul do not. In the spiritual process the mystical marriage can only be accomplished after this inequality is remedied. The progressive purifying and strengthening eventually enables the soul to unite to God in sameness, as God's equal or counterpart.

At times, during our earthly journey, this ongoing spiritual relationship may be without sensible feelings but, just as in earthly marriage, the prime ingredient is LOVING FAITH-FULNESS. A commitment has been made for life which is not based merely on enjoyable feelings. There will be good times and bad times in every relationship but, when we are aware of its worth and our love is deep enough, we are willing to make an effort and not run from our commitment.

Marriage, for those called to that vocation, is a school of sanctity. St. Paul likens the process to the collective transformation of the world which is gradually evolving with each evolving soul, and will reach spiritual completion in the fullness of God's appointed time. "For this reason, a man must leave his father and mother and be joined to his wife, and the two will become one body. This mystery has many implications; but I am saying it applies to Christ and the Church" (Ephesians 5:31).

In recent years, through the influence of Eastern spirituality, the terms "meditation" and "contemplation" are often used interchangeably. However, in the ancient Christian tradition, "meditation" was generally considered to be the prelude to "contemplation." The novices of a monastic community, most of whom could not read, would listen to a Scripture passage, memorize it, and turn it over and over in their minds, ruminating, digesting, and extracting from the passage all of the hidden meanings they could find while performing their manual duties. This was considered "discursive meditation," in which the mind was actively involved in the gaining of knowledge about God through its own efforts of rational consideration. During this process the mind was encouraged to wander and ramble, searching for meaningful ideas and concepts about God.

Later, in quiet prayer, when physical activity had ceased, the novices would let all of the insights they had discovered sink deep within to their center, where God dwells. Here the active mind was stilled, the faculties quieted, and the soul "rested" in God, passively receptive and open to whatever God wished to provide. "Enough for me to keep my soul tranquil and quiet like a child in its mother's arms" (Psalm 131:2). This was considered "acquired" contemplation, which could be practiced by all people, regardless of their state in life.

The habit of acquired contemplation was referred to as the "prayer of recollection" by St. Teresa of Avila. Through her firsthand experience of the soul's journey to divine union and mystical marriage, Teresa was inspired by God to provide insight, explanations, and encouragement for the benefit of other contemplative souls.

"This prayer is called 'recollection,' because the soul collects its faculties together and enters within itself to be with its God. And its divine Master comes more quickly to teach it and give it the prayer of quiet than He would through any other method it might use.

"You must understand that this recollection is not something supernatural, but that it is something we can desire and achieve ourselves with the help of God — for without this help we can do nothing, not even have a good thought. This recollection is not a silence of the faculties: it is an enclosure of the faculties within the soul" *(Way of Perfection,* St. Teresa of Avila, ch. 28:4, 29:4).

What Teresa called "the prayer of quiet" is the beginning of supernatural prayer or "infused" contemplation, which is instilled by God. Teresa believed that many spiritually prepared people, while meditating, are gently led by God into the prayer of quiet. "This prayer, then, is a little spark of the Lord's true love which He begins to enkindle in the soul; and He desires that the soul grow in the understanding of what this love accompanied by delight is" (Life, St. Teresa of Avila, ch. 15:4).

St. Teresa (and her friend and fellow Carmelite St. John of the Cross) believed that many souls could reach not only the prayer of quiet, but the prayer of union and the grace of divine transformation during their earthly life, if they were willing to endure the cross, "the narrow gate" indicated by Jesus. "This little spark is the sign or the pledge God gives to this soul that He now chooses it for great things if it will prepare itself to receive them. This spark is a great gift, much more so than I can express. As I say, I know many souls that reach this stage, but to me it is a terrible pity that those that pass beyond, as they should, are so few" (Ibid., ch. 15:5).

The early Christians considered contemplation the natural fulfillment of every Christian life. This attitude continued for the first fifteen centuries of Christianity, until it began to be suppressed by the Church. It would seem that part of the problem was a misunderstanding of the word "contemplation," for it not only covers many levels or degrees of prayer, but also what we can prepare for and expect, and what is entirely God's doing.

"Contemplation was regarded as extraordinary and identified with extraordinary phenomena, in other words, something miraculous to be admired from a safe distance, but left alone as dangerous, full of pitfalls, and not something to which the ordinary Christian, layman, priest or religious, should aspire . . . it was against humility" (Thomas Keating, OCSO, America, April 1978).

This description seems to indicate the more intense type of infused contemplation communicated by God, a manner of divine intervention which is not that of the ordinary. The contemplation referred to as extraordinary is not acquired contemplation, nor the prayer of quiet which God ordinarily infuses drop by drop without unusual occurrences. It is true that no one should aspire to extraordinary experiences, for no one knows the mind of God. It is also true that if God wills to intervene in a more powerful way, He will do so whether or not the soul is consciously seeking Him, or "worthy," since this intervention is not a reward for "good deeds." The examples in the lives of many Saints, especially St. Paul, affirm this. The massive infusions which may, or may not, be accompanied by mystical phenomena are entirely God's prerogative, and are the imparting of divine life in a more concentrated or instantaneous way.

All of the Saints did not experience visions, raptures, or the other supernatural phenomena which, in the minds of many people, have often been associated with sanctity. But the same state of divine transformation was reached by all of the Saints, regardless of whether or not they experienced unusual manifestations. "Nothing is impossible for God," and He works in each soul according to His plan. The spiritual development of some of the Saints was such that it drew attention, while others were completely hidden from worldly eyes during their earthly life, and known but to God.

During the brief life of St. Therese, there were no unusual spiritual experiences to catch the attention of the other nuns in the Carmelite convent at Lisieux. In fact, at her death at the age of twenty-four, some of the nuns who had lived with her wondered what could possibly be said of her in her death notice, since she lived such a brief, and supposedly uneventful, life. In the simplicity of her life and her faithfulness to "the little way of spiritual childhood," Therese affirmed the Gospel message that the call to holiness is an open invitation to everyone, regardless of their state in life.

God's irresistible power is always at work in the world, whether or not we are aware of it. Divine love is a powerful force which God ordinarily "feeds" to souls drop by drop throughout their lifetime, interspersed with sufferings and setbacks, to gradually condition them to bear the full weight of His glory — divine transformation. For most people, this ongoing process does not interrupt or interfere with their day-to-day activities, but enhances them.

When God chooses certain individuals to be used as instruments in some particular aspect of His divine plan, He gives them a "crash course" of divine enlightenment, an accelerated form of the same spiritual development that everyone else experiences. By way of this more powerful infused contemplation, God brings them to the fullness of divine transformation in a shorter period of time. This divinizing process is not just for their own benefit, but to change them into "other Christs" working in the world for the good of their brothers and sisters. "I have been crucified with Christ. It is now no longer I that live, but Christ lives in me" (Galatians 2:20).

The force of divine love is such that, when it comes in other than the ordinary, gradual way, human nature is not always equipped to withstand it, similar to the way an unexpected surge of power might damage our appliances or cause temporary outages. One hot summer afternoon a violent thunderstorm arose, and lightning flashed very near our house. The television set suddenly came on, by-passing the on/off switch which, after that, never worked. To turn the set on or off the plug had to be put in or taken out of the outlet.

Since I had always seen an analogy between spirituality and electricity (even the terms — light, power, generation, transformation, etc.), I asked my husband, who is with the electric company, for a simple explanation. He said that for current to flow through a circuit there must be voltage (force), a conductor (wire), and a closed circuit or complete path. When the path is interrupted, such as an open switch, it is not a complete path. The voltage (force) is there — across the open contacts of the switch there is a voltage difference — but there is no current flowing because the contacts of the switch are separated by air, which is normally a non-conductor. Normal voltage is not enough to "arc" across or "bridge the gap," but an unusually powerful surge could arc across the open contacts of the switch, even through the air. To increase the voltage, with no change in resistance, would cause an increased current flow. Conversely, even with no increase in voltage, but by lowering the resistance, there would also be a more powerful flow of current.

To me there seemed to be a simile between the activity of electricity and God's activity in the soul. When we initiate the action (acquired contemplation) we spiritually "close the switch" making a complete path, or channel, for the Divine outpouring. As we gradually adapt our will to God's will throughout our life's journey, we "lower our resistance" by becoming more receptive, enabling the Divine Current to be infused in an ever-increasing way (instilled infused contemplation), just as relaxing a "pinch" on a hose would allow a more forceful flow of water even though there was no increase in water pressure. The powerful force of divine love is waiting to inundate us, but is divinely controlled to adapt to each soul's spiritual readiness and capacity to receive. God is ever solicitous for the soul's welfare.

When God takes the initiative (accelerated infused contemplation) it would be as if the Divine Force suddenly became extraordinarily high, so powerful that it created an arc across the open switch, causing the current to flow through air. Air, normally a non-conductor, would be forced to conduct through the power of this overwhelming force. A lamp on this circuit would shine more brilliantly than usual, but the bulb could certainly not last as long as it would have under average conditions. This was the experience of some of the saints surprised or seized by God, but nevertheless responding in love and cooperating with divine will.

"I, Daniel, alone saw the apparition. . . . I heard him speak, and at the sound of his voice I fell unconscious to the ground. . . . He said then, 'Daniel, do not be afraid.' . . . And as he spoke to me I felt strong again and said, 'Let my Lord speak, You have given me strength' " (Daniel 10:7, 9, 12, 19).

Which soul God chooses as His instrument, and why He chooses, will always be a mystery. But we can see that "accelerated" infused contemplation is not something that the soul should seek or is able to obtain through its own efforts, for it is entirely God's doing. On the other hand, "acquired" contemplation (or the prayer of recollection), and a gradual "instilled" infused contemplation (beginning with the prayer of quiet), are possible for all who are willing to devote the time and effort necessary for an ever-deepening relationship with the Indwelling God.

Although all prayer is meant to be contemplative, in that the mind and heart should be lifted to God, there are two distinctive characteristics of what is considered true contemplative prayer. They are first, a change of focus, and second, the purpose or goal of contemplative prayer.

The change of focus is directed toward seeking God within, the God Who is "my other self," and "Nearer to me than I am to myself" (St. Augustine), as opposed to seeking a God Who is outside oneself, distant, or far away. The contemplative's emphasis and concentration converge on the Indwelling God in the depths of the soul.

"All the harm comes from not truly understanding that He is near, but in imagining Him as far away" (*Way of Perfection*, St. Teresa of Avila, ch. 29:5).

The second distinguishing aspect of contemplative prayer is its primary goal of union with God. Again, St. Teresa of Avila has encouraging advice to offer prayerful souls yearning for an experience of the Indwelling God here and now: "I would like to know a way of explaining how this holy fellowship with our Companion, the Saint of saints, may be experienced without any hindrance to the solitude enjoyed between the soul and its Spouse when the soul desires to enter this paradise within itself to be with its God and close the door to all the world. . . . Since nothing is learned without a little effort, consider, for the love of God, as well employed the attention you give to this method of prayer. I know, if you try, that within a year, or perhaps half a year, you will acquire it, by the favor of God" (Ibid., ch. 29:4, 8).

It is significant for our spiritual lives that Jesus usually asked for some small effort from His followers before He performed His miracles. The exercise of free will, in which love resides, was required. God does not plan to transform the world, or individual souls, through miracles alone. He expects cooperation, just as parents, for the sake of the child's development, do not do everything themselves but expect some effort from the child.

The blind man was told to wash the mud from his eyes before he could see; the bread and fish had to be brought to Jesus before He fed the multitude; and, at Cana, the earthen vessels had to be filled with water which Jesus intended to transform into wine. God is used to creating something out of nothing and did not need these things in order to perform miracles.

Did you ever wonder what the people who were involved in these situations were thinking when Jesus made His requests? At the wedding feast of Cana, when the servant was asked to dip some water from the jar and take it to the wine steward to taste, he must have felt some embarrassment. The servant knew what it was, for he had filled the jars himself. At the risk of looking foolish, the servant did what Jesus requested and, through his humble obedience and trust, he witnessed a miracle when most of the people at the feast were not even aware that anything out of the ordinary had taken place. "God humbles the soul only in order to exalt it" (John of the Cross). It is only after we have been emptied, which requires our willingness to endure, that we can be filled, which is all God's doing.

"Actions speak louder than words" and, since action requires some effort, it is usually a clearer indication of love, trust, and a deeper faith commitment. God asks only for small deeds that are possible for everyone. The very simplicity of the deed itself is part of our humbling experience. We are made fully aware that it is not our insignificant actions that bring about miracles, but the power of God that is at work in us and in the world. We just have to be available and willing.

To trust in the promises of Christ, and to act in everyday life according to the reality of that belief, is living faith. In regular contemplative prayer we learn to wait trustingly and patiently in the presence of God, with or without consolations, whether in dryness, or in emptiness and tears, convinced He is near until, with a glance, He turns the water of our tears into the wine of His love. Then we too can say with the steward, "Lord, You have kept the best wine until now" (John 2:10).

3

Spiritual Preparations for Contemplative Prayer

St. Teresa of Avila considered contemplative prayer more as "relationship" than "recitation."

"Whoever has not begun the practice of [contemplative] prayer, I beg for the love of the Lord not to go without so great a good. There is nothing here to fear but only something to desire. Even if there be no great progress, or much effort in reaching such perfection as to deserve the favors and mercies God bestows on the more generous, at least a person will come to understand the road leading to heaven. And if he perseveres, I trust then in the mercy of God, who never fails to repay anyone who has taken Him for a friend. FOR MENTAL PRAYER IN MY OPINION IS NOTHING ELSE THAN AN INTIMATE SHARING BETWEEN FRIENDS; IT MEANS TAKING TIME FREQUENTLY TO BE ALONE WITH HIM WHO WE KNOW LOVES US. In order that love be true and the friendship endure, the wills of the friends must be in accord" (*Life*, St. Teresa of Avila, ch. 8:5).

"A much greater love for and confidence in this Lord began to develop in me when I saw Him as one with whom I could converse so continually. . . . I can speak with Him as with a friend, even though He is Lord" (*Ibid.*, ch. 37:5).

Through the contemplative relationship, friendship with the Lord grows into love. Contemplative prayer means "being present" to the Lord; it is not something that we "do" or "achieve," but a way of simply "being with" and being "intensely aware of" the Lord.

It is important to have a quiet, private place of our own for prayer. It could be a room, or even a corner of a room, perhaps just turning a chair toward a window if there is a peaceful scene. If there is no worthwhile view, the chair could be turned toward a cross or picture that evokes a sense of the holy. St. Teresa, instructing her nuns on beginning interior prayer, advised them to obtain "an image or painting of this Lord that is to your liking" *(Ibid.,* ch. 27:9). Soon, as it becomes a habit, the prayer place itself becomes a help in establishing a sense of the presence of God, and the turning of a chair can symbolize our inner turning (metanoia) of the heart and mind to God. As it becomes habitual, interior prayer can be practiced any place, such as travelling by plane or bus, during any free time, like waiting for a friend.

Prayer supports, such as using an image, a scene, music, or a particular place, are not ends in themselves but a means to the end, which is God. There is a natural inclination to cling to what is "known," and which may provide the soul with consolations or comfortable feelings. Detachment includes the proper attitude towards spiritual possessions as well as material for, eventually, God will ask the soul to walk without support, and trust only in Him.

"These considerations, forms, and methods of meditation are necessary to beginners that the soul may be enamored and fed through the senses, as we shall point out later. They are suitable as the remote means to union with God, which beginners must ordinarily use for the attainment of their goal and the abode of spiritual repose. Yet these means must not be so used that a person always employs them and never advances, for then he would never achieve his goal, which is unlike the remote means and unproportioned to it — just as none of the steps on a flight of stairs has any resemblance to the goal at the top toward which they are the means. If a man in climbing them does not leave each one behind until there are no more, or if he should want to stay on one of them, he would never reach the level and peaceful room at the top" (The Ascent of Mt. Carmel, St. John of the Cross, Bk. II, ch. 12:5).

A comfortable position for prayer is necessary. To be uncomfortable will increase distractions, and cause a constant shifting of position. If we become too comfortable, it is easy to fall asleep. The recommended posture is to sit upright in a straight-backed chair, with feet resting flat on the floor, and hands resting in the lap, but if some other position is preferred or seems natural, then it is right for the individual. If gazing at an image, a scene, or a cross is helpful in collecting the thoughts by all means do so. In time, most people find that closing the eyes will happen automatically, so don't force it. Be as gentle with the self as with a dear friend. The hoped-for state is to be relaxed, but alert and aware. "Be still and know [experience] that I am God" (Psalm 46:10).

A notebook, for jotting down any ideas that form immediately after prayer, can be invaluable. The Spirit more easily reaches the conscious mind during the relaxed state of the body in prayer, and often provides helpful insights or expressions of love. One's own inspirations may eventually be the best preparation for prayer. Since each soul is uniquely led, notes are also a help in discerning the way that the Spirit is guiding the soul, and for discussions with spiritual friends or director.

Distractions will always be a part of the human condition. The important thing is not to be overly upset by them, for then the agitation disrupts the inner tranquility that is necessary. "You cannot begin to recollect yourselves by force but only by gentleness, if your recollection is going to be more continual" (Interior Castle, St. Teresa of Avila, II:1).

Our responsibility is to be faithful to prayer and give

our regular time to the Lord each day; the rest is up to God. If the entire prayer period is filled with distractions or aridity, it does not matter! God looks at our hearts and sees our intentions. The mind should not dwell on the distractions, but be brought gently back to God each time the mind wanders, by a loving phrase or word, looking again at an image, or just an inner recalling of a sense of the holy. Almost everyone remembers a time or place in which there was a vivid sense of the presence of God. After the experience, many people may think that they have been mistaken, and begin to have doubts about its validity. These experiences remain in the depths of memory, however, and are very often a true experience of the Indwelling God, Who "delights to be with the children of men." To recall these graced moments helps to restore our inner tranquility and remind us of His loving presence.

The busy mind is used to being active. Teresa of Avila described this flitting about of the thoughts as resembling "a mad woman loose in the house." It could also be pictured as an inquisitive child, running from one thing to the other. For the soul to abandon prayer to run after the imagination or the intellect would only cause further distractions. Teresa advises, "One should leave the intellect go and surrender oneself into the arms of love" (Ibid., IV:3, 8).

Contemplative prayer has also been pictured as watching a peaceful stream flowing by, sparkling in the sunlight. From time to time there may be leaves, branches, or other debris floating by on the surface of the stream -- the distractions. They are observed, but it is not necessary to do anything about them; just remain calm and serene as they pass. If real problems come to mind, which often happens when we are relaxed, just make a mental note that they will be dealt with immediately after the prayer session, and do so, but do not interrupt the prayer (unless, of course, there is an emergency).

Spiritual reading is an important part of the soul's development, and is very beneficial to the practice of prayer. It inspires and stirs the heart, helping it to soar more readily to God. "It is also a great help to take a good book written in the vernacular in order to recollect one's thoughts and pray well . . . little by little accustom the soul with coaxing and skill not to grow discouraged" *(Way of Perfection*, St. Teresa of Avila, ch. 27:10).

For our part, acquired contemplation requires the effort of spiritual preparation, discipline, and forming the right intentions, thereby conditioning oneself to receive whatever God wills, as these attitudes and dispositions before God become habitual. Everything else is in God's hands.

DISCIPLINE includes:

Setting aside a regular time and place for silence and solitude.

Faithfulness in keeping our commitment to pray, regardless of whether or not we FEEL like it.

Realizing our responsibility. We are expected to cooperate in the development of the divine treasure entrusted to our care. We should not be fooled, by ourselves or others, into thinking we are engaging in some extravagance of "doing nothing" or "wasting time" by practicing contemplative prayer. In the spiritual area, "being" is more important than "doing." This spiritual principle does not imply a "do-nothing" attitude in the other areas of earthly life. If anything, the contemplative, growing in divine love and awareness, develops a deeper care and concern for the world, and recognizes that "We are all His children" (Acts 17:28).

Focusing attention, the practice of being present to God within, as opposed to thinking of God as far away, requires the habitual calming of our faculties, stilling the busy mind, and gathering the wayward affections to a point, that "still point" deep within, where we know the Lord is always patiently waiting. "Your spouse never takes His eyes off you" *(Way of Perfection*, St. Teresa of Avila, ch. 26:3).

INTENTION includes:

Seek the Giver, not the gifts, seeking God for Himself alone, not solely for prayer experiences or spiritual consolations. There is no such thing as "good" or "bad" prayer; it cannot be graded according to how prayer makes us feel. What happens or does not happen during prayer time is not as important as what we are becoming — "like" God. How we live and act the rest of the day is more indicative of authentic spiritual growth than any consolations that may occur in prayer. "By their fruits you shall know them" (Matthew 12:33). "For perfection as well as its reward does not consist in spiritual delights but in greater love and in deeds done with greater justice and truth" *(Interior Castle,* St. Teresa of Avila, III:2, 10).

Desire to be one with God, a union of love brought about by the gradual refining of our will, until it is compatible with divine will. Desire itself is a grace from God and draws Him to the soul.

"The desire for God is the preparation for union with Him. . . . In the first place it should be known that if a person is seeking God, his Beloved is seeking him much more. . . . If a soul directs to God its loving desires . . . by which He draws it and makes it run after Him . . . the soul is so delicately and purely prepared that it merits union with Him and substantial transformation in all its faculties" (St. John of the Cross, *Living Flame of Love,* St. 3: 26, 28).

Becoming like God, growing in all of His attributes through absorbing them and consciously living them, thereby making them a real part of us. Divine traits must be practiced in order for them to become interiorized and effect a permanent change.

ATTITUDE includes:

Belief in the Indwelling God and His love for us — FAITH response. A life of prayer is faith in action. Virtues strengthen through use.

Patient, expectant waiting — living HOPE in promises of Christ. "To the one who loves Me I will reveal Myself."

Surrender of self, returning LOVE for LOVE beyond sense-feelings. "Here am I, Lord; I come to do Your will." Self-giving response to God's self-giving love, willing to be instrument in His hands, accepting God's will, not trying to convince Him of ours. Free will is essence of God Who is complete freedom, but human will must be brought into alignment with divine will and be wholly compatible. Acceptance makes us willing to give up control in the spiritual area of our lives, for God alone forms the soul. Oneness of will brings Divine Union, Transformation, Spiritual Marriage.

Humility — TRUTH. Self-knowledge is required through every stage of the soul's interior journey.

Openness and receptivity; approachable and vulnerable; adaptable, flexible, not rigid; willing to change, to be led by God with a childlike trust and confidence.

Gratitude for all of God's gifts, His love, the beauty of creation, human life — through which we grow into divine life. (Each day begins with a miracle: I am alive!)

Awareness of being in the Presence of God. Listening with the heart develops inner perception, intuitive "knowing," "seeing," for God is a hidden God and comes to us in ordinary ways.

In "acquired" contemplation, God still does the work of forming the soul, but the initial efforts and spiritual preparation are up to each individual. As with Jesus performing His miracles, the soul sees that it is not its own insignificant actions that bring about its growth in divine love; it is all God's work. "Unless the Lord builds the house, they labor in vain who build it" (Psalm 127).

Living the divine attributes shapes the soul in the divine "posture" or attitude. ("As the twig is bent so shall it grow.") God does not hold Himself distant from His children, but bends to our level, as a father gets down on the floor to play with his little ones. To approach others from the vantage point of humility and love is to see Christ more clearly in the eyes of those we serve.

Sometimes the infusion of divine gifts is experienced by the senses, and at other times it proceeds completely unnoticed. Therefore, to be overly concerned with temporary consolations or experiences in prayer can be distracting, for it tends to focus our attention more on the "self" than on God. Our minds and hearts must be attentive to God, aligned with His will, receptive, silent, and still, while God is transferring His spiritual "goods" from His abundance to our emptiness. Divine gifts cannot be grasped or demanded; the soul can only gratefully receive.

Oneness with God in love and eventual participation in the love relationship of the Trinity is the reason for our creation and the fulfillment of God's plan. Following the contemplative path enables us to enjoy, to some extent, this gift of participated being even during our earthly existence.

"The soul's center is God. When it has reached God with all the capacity of its being and the strength of its operation and inclination, it will have attained to its final and deepest center in God, it will know, love, and enjoy God with all its might. . . . For the will of the two is one will, and thus God's operation and the soul's is one. . . . Having been made One with God, the soul is somehow GOD THROUGH PARTICIPATION" (Living Flame of Love, St. John of the Cross, St. 1:12; 3:78).

The writings of St. John of the Cross reaffirm the Good News of Scripture: "In making these gifts, He has given us the guarantee of something very great and wonderful to come: THROUGH THEM YOU WILL BE ABLE TO SHARE THE DIVINE NATURE" (2 Peter 1:4).

This spiritual "becoming" woven through the fabric of our everyday lives is not always evident. To remain still and silent in God's presence increases our inner awareness, develops a taste for the holy, and helps us to recognize the "still, small voice," then cooperate and re-

64

spond to God's will. Gradually we learn to let go of self-will, which enables us to offer our "fiat" necessary for union. The willingness to abandon ourselves humbly to God, without being overly concerned with "results," is basic to our spiritual development and should be our attitude of prayer. "Leave the soul in God's hands, let Him do whatever He wants with it, with the greatest disinterest about your own benefit as is possible and the greatest resignation to the will of God" (*Interior Castle*, St. Teresa of Avila, IV:3, 6).

Two people, deeply in love, enjoy being together in silence sensing each other's presence and their inner oneness. When this happens in prayer, between God and the soul, the active mind may feel left out. The human mind is used to receiving information, considering or reflecting upon it, and then digesting and storing it. When it is divine knowledge or enlightenment, which is present and increasing through growth in divine love, the usual process is circumvented. The busy mind may try to distract or interrupt the soul, or complain as Martha did of Mary, since it is not quite able to understand this divine placidity.

"For while the faculties are dead or asleep, love remains alive. And the Lord ordains that the soul function so wonderfully, without its understanding how, that it is made one, in great purity, with the very Lord of love, Who is God. For no one hinders the soul, neither senses nor faculties (I mean intellect and memory), nor is the will aware of itself" (*Meditations on the Song of Songs*, St. Teresa of Avila, ch. 6:4).

"Since the wisdom of this contemplation is the language of God to the soul, of Pure Spirit to the spirit alone, all that is less than spirit, such as the sensory, fails to perceive it. Consequently this wisdom is secret to the senses; they have neither the knowledge nor ability to speak of it, nor do they even desire to do so because it is beyond words" (*The Dark Night*, St. John of the Cross, Book II, ch. 17:4).

4

Mystical Knowledge and Rational Knowledge

"I prayed, and understanding was given me. . . . Wisdom is quicker to move than any motion: she is so pure, she pervades and permeates all things. She is a breath of the power of God, pure emanation of the glory of the Almighty . . . a reflection of the eternal light, untarnished mirror of God's active power, image of His goodness. Although alone, she can do all: herself unchanging, she makes all things new. In each generation she passes into holy souls, she makes them friends of God and prophets" (Wisdom 7:7, 24).

"Mysticism — doctrine that knowledge of spiritual truths may be attained intuitively."

"Intuition — the immediate knowing or learning of something without the conscious use of reasoning."

There are two kinds of knowledge — "rational" knowledge and "mystical" knowledge. "Rational" knowledge is gained through our conscious effort; it is the work of the created intellect. Through the use of our senses, reading, studying, and hearing talks, facts or information "about" God is gathered and stored in the memory.

"Mystical" knowledge is not knowledge "about" God, but God Himself that is apprehended intuitively. Through the activity of God in our deepest center, mystical knowledge is absorbed from within, by-passing the created senses.

"He who would go to God relying upon natural ability and reasoning will not be very spiritual. There are some who think that by pure force and the activity of the senses, which of itself is lowly and no more than natural, they can reach the strength and height of the supernatural spirit. One does not attain to this peak without suppressing and leaving aside the activity of the senses. . . .

"Pure contemplation lies in receiving. It is impossible for this highest wisdom and language of God, which is contemplation, to be received in anything less than a spirit that is silent and detached from discursive knowledge and gratification.

"This wisdom is loving, tranquil, solitary, peaceful, mild, and an inebriator of the spirit, by which the soul feels tenderly and gently wounded and carried away, without knowing by whom, nor from where, nor how. The reason is that this wisdom is communicated without the soul's own activity" (Living Flame of Love, St. John of the Cross, St. 2:14; 3:37, 38).

Through a kind of "spiritual osmosis" the soul is gradually absorbing God, by silent time spent in each other's presence.

"Osmosis — Gr. osmos — impulse; the tendency of fluids to pass through a somewhat porous membrane so as to equalize concentrations on both sides."

In spiritual osmosis the concentration of divine life, love, and knowledge, through the impulse of God, gradually becomes absorbed, equalized, and fully balanced in the divine/human spirit.

This divine activity is far beyond the capacity of the created human intellect to observe or evaluate, and proceeds regardless of whether or not the created senses or feelings are involved.

"Contemplation is also termed mystical theology, meaning the secret or hidden knowledge of God. In contemplation God teaches the soul very quietly and secretly, without its knowing how, without the sound of words, and without the help of any bodily or spiritual faculty, in silence and quietude, in darkness to all sensory and natural things. Some spiritual persons call this contemplation knowing by unknowing" *(Spiritual Canticle,* St. John of the Cross, St. 39:12).

"It is written in the prophets: 'They will all be taught by God' " (John 6:45).

To be taught by God, and not through our own conscious efforts, may be for us a completely new approach to spiritual growth. It is the reason for the spiritual emphasis on becoming a "little child," and allowing God to lead and form the soul, remaining passively receptive and not interfering with this delicate work.

In the beginning of the spiritual journey, this is often difficult for people to become accustomed to, especially those who are "take charge" types. Even those who are not often resist the idea of giving up control. We hesitate on the brink of this mysterious unknown, for we are used to proceeding through blocks of time schedules, semesters or years, during which our "performance" is graded or evaluated, and in which we are able to observe our progress and achievements, and thereby enjoy a sense of satisfaction and pride of "accomplishment."

But our human "measuring rods" are useless in the spiritual world where "the last is first"; the "greatest among you is the servant of all"; the "weak confound the strong"; and "a little child shall lead them." In this spiritual land it is necessary to let that spiritual, eternal child, which is in each one of us, lead us to the Father.

"To reach a new and unknown land and travel unknown roads, a man cannot be guided by his own knowledge, rather he has doubts about his own knowledge and seeks the guidance of others. Obviously he cannot reach new territory nor attain this added knowledge if he does not take these new and unknown roads and abandon those familiar ones. . . . The soul too, when it advances, walks in darkness and unknowing. Since God, as we said, is the master and guide of the soul, this blind man, it can truly rejoice" (*The Dark Night*, St. John of the Cross, Bk. II, ch. 16:8).

If, through self-knowledge, we know ourselves, and have gained some idea of the omnipotence of God, it will come as no surprise that we cannot immediately comprehend divine wisdom.

"How rich are the depths of God — how deep His wisdom and knowledge — and how impossible to penetrate His motives or understand His methods! Who could ever know the mind of the Lord?" (Romans 11:33).

In the silent absorption of contemplation we wait, experiencing God through love without attempting to analyze, question, or measure, as He fills us with His own divine life. In the stillness we train the mirror of our souls upon God, and the mirror-image becomes progressively clearer and more indelible.

Mystical knowledge is both love and wisdom. Love is of the "essence" of God, not of the created, and is therefore able to immediately unite with God; but Divine Wisdom is incomprehensible to the created mind and is not always fully understood at the moment that it is received. Part of the suffering of the "dark night" is that the faculties are not able to function in their accustomed manner. Love has to love, and reason has to reason. Both are proceeding according to their nature, but the created needs time to grasp and absorb the Divine, as the body needs time to digest and assimilate food.

Love IS God, of His very nature, and is able to surmount matter and merge with God in sameness, while the understanding lags behind. Love transcends the mere human way of proceeding, and goes out of itself to God in a kind of "quantum leap." Love is like the rope of the mountain climber which grasps a new peak, then supports the struggling, created intellect while it "hangs suspended" for a time. When understanding "catches up," the "rope of love" again flings higher. Created consciousness slowly assimilates the divine knowledge with which it has been filled, before it arrives at that place to which love, uncreated spirit, has effortlessly leaped.

Love effects change; information, without love, does not. Knowledge, even spiritual knowledge, of itself is not growth inducing. Divine transformation does not require knowledge equal to God's, but it does require equal love. True spiritual growth is accomplished through humble openness to the Divine infusion. Love contains all that God is and, eventually, all that the soul is, as the soul's capacity is strengthened and expanded to fulfill its divine destiny of being equal to God.

Spiritual writers have said that information plus experience equals wisdom.

"Experience must be restored to its rightful place in theology; doctrinal truth and a life of prayer must be wedded again. Theology begins with experience, and experience reflected upon produces theology. . . .

"If we stop short of the deep inner stuff of religion, chances are we'll become either fanatics or skeptics. The deep inner stuff of religion is called the mystical life. It consists primarily of the contemplation of truth. Contemplation is a supremely human and intuitive gaze on truth" (*The Human Adventure*, Fr. William McNamara, OCD, pp. 17, 100).

"You will learn the truth and the truth will make you free" (John 8:32).

In every area of our lives, in order to communicate we must know the language. God's language is "the silent language of love," which requires the ability to listen with the heart. Learning the language of divine love puts us in touch not only with God, but with all those who are close to Him, both in heaven and on earth. From time to time during our earthly journey we may glimpse, at the edge of perception, the radiant beauty of another's soul in the blinding flash of a "Transfiguration experience." At the sudden recognition of Spirit and Spirit, an answering flame leaps up spontaneously from our depths.

"Master, it is wonderful for us to be here!" (Luke 9:33).

"The moment your greeting reached my ears, the child in my womb leapt for joy!" (John 21:7).

Through the Indwelling, Divinity smiles out at us from other eyes and speaks through their mouths, sometimes so directly and immediately that the encounter and its significance can neither be mistaken nor denied.

"Did not our hearts burn within us as He talked to us on the road?" (Luke 24:32).

Through the ever-growing intimacy of the prayer relationship, Christ becomes "familiar" to the soul, and is therefore more easily recognized regardless of the outward "disguise." Contemplative awareness is necessary in order to recognize Him for "Our God is a hidden God." Because of obvious human weaknesses and failings, the clearer, deeper perception of the soul is needed to "see" the paradox of the Divine within the human, whether it be in ourselves, or in our sisters and brothers. The contemplative spirit keeps us open and receptive, with a sense of wonder and awe at the reality of the presence of God "shining diaphanously at the heart of creation" (Chardin). The contemplative remains a spiritual child, young at heart, regardless of the passing years.

To the prayerful soul loving and generous enough to give God the time, and humble and willing enough to listen and change, Christ will come again. "I will not leave you orphans: I will come back to you" (John 14:16).

In the depths of contemplation as we sense His gaze upon us, irresistibly drawing our souls to "Come, follow Me," we are moved to respond. From time to time we are called to temporarily leave our "nets," the entanglements of the world, the trivia with which we have become so caught up, too many possessions that in time "own" us, prejudices not worthy of the divine intelligence that God shares with us, and false images of God or ourselves that tend to block out the Divine Light. To know (experience) the depths of God, we must first know (experience) the depths of ourselves, and the dark emptiness of the creature without God's light and love. "The soul is like an empty vessel waiting to be filled" *(Spiritual Canticle,* St. John of the Cross, St. 9:6).

5

The Soul's Journey to Union With God

Our existence is a progressive, uninterrupted "becoming," which begins at conception and has no ending. "Before I formed you in the womb I knew you; before you came to birth I consecrated you" (Jeremiah 1:4).

At conception God infuses each human being with a "spark" from the flame of His own Divine Life, a fusing of the divine and human similar to the Incarnation of Jesus — with one important difference. Jesus is God by nature, and freely chose to take on a created, human nature. We receive both the divine, eternal, uncreated, and the human, finite, created as gifts from God. From the instant of our conception the golden thread that ties it all together is the Divine Life of God within us. "In Him we live, and move, and have our being" (Acts 17:28).

Our divine "spark" contains the seed of ALL that God is since God is not subject to division. All of the divine attributes are meant to be nourished and developed in the human spirit, bringing the human to a spiritual height, depth, and expanse capable of assimilating the divine, and becoming "equal" to God. This interior transition is the purpose of religion, contemplative prayer, religious rules and rituals, in fact, of our very existence itself.

"Accordingly, souls possess the same goods by participation that the Son possesses by nature. As a result they are truly GODS BY PARTICIPATION, EQUALS AND

COMPANIONS OF GOD" (*Spiritual Canticle,* St. John of the Cross, St. 39:6).

Once called into being, we can never be uncreated. The divine/human spirit within us can no more be separated than the physical elements of flesh, blood, and genes of the parents can be removed from the child. Spirit-led to gradual awareness during its time on earth, the soul recognizes, absorbs, and "becomes like" God in an indissoluble union. God first loves us into "being" then, through our heart-to-heart relationship with Him and the people and events of our daily life, He loves us into "becoming."

The beginning soul often delights in the "honeymoon" stages of prayer with its sensible consolations. God first draws souls to Him through the created senses to detach their affections from earthly pleasures and acquire a taste for the heavenly. Union of God and the soul, however, requires a purgation which cannot be accomplished in the "honeymoon" stage, and so the soul will be led through many deserts and oases. In the "desert" we may experience dryness, aridity, a sense of the absence of God; then from time to time, we are aware of being enveloped by a loving Presence, touches of love, or peaceful consolations; this is the "oasis." Since we know that the fusion of the divine/human spirit occurs at the very beginning of our existence, God can never truly be "absent" from the soul. What is absent are the feelings of delight that the prayerful soul once enjoyed.

Any description of the spiritual dimension of existence is always an attempt to express the inexpressible, and is far beyond what we are able to explain in human language. We speak of God's love or life "growing" in us, and of God "moving near" or "being absent" from the soul. These are all descriptions of our feelings, or how we experience the divine activity in our depths. Any growth and change that occur take place in our perception of God and His love, and our ability to respond and grow in that love. But it is necessary for us as humans to make use of human means of expression. Spiritual experiences must be reflected upon and articulated. This process aids the discernment of how God is working in each particular soul, affirms the reality of the experience, and strengthens and encourages the soul in preparation for further development. In this respect small prayer communities of like-minded individuals within the larger Church community are highly beneficial for mutual encouragement, spiritual growth, and prayerful support. Small groups of "one heart and one soul" (Acts 4:32) provide the environment which fosters divine intimacy.

Human existence, although continuous, consists of three distinct stages, like a rocket, the soul's thrust being the force of Divine Life and Love within us. In the womb, the first stage, united with God but unaware, we develop and are born into the world. In the second stage, earthly life, our awareness of God develops and our ability to receive love and respond in love. Growth in divine love and conformity to divine will forms the soul's unique reflection of God, which is born into eternal life, the third and final stage. When the "vehicle" of the body has served its purpose and is "jettisoned," the soul returns to its Source, its Homeland, and a God-like existence for all eternity. At the end of time as we know it, we have the promise of a general Resurrection, but the particulars of our "glorified body" are still a mystery.

The infant develops in the womb until it is capable of existing on earth. The soul is meant to develop on earth until it is able to exist in heaven. If it has not developed as it should, it will not have the capacity for the divine, which is necessary in order to participate in the God-life of heaven. God does not "send" us to heaven or hell. What we experience is the result of our spiritual condition, formed through our own free will and decision making over a lifetime.

If, through some magic potion, a two-year-old could

suddenly be thirty years old, he would not be able to cope or participate in an adult world. He would have no idea of how to think, act, or relate on an adult level. He might have been able to avoid some pain and suffering, but he would not have gained the wisdom that day-to-day living and experience brings.

It is the same with spiritual development. There is no such thing as "innocent suffering," since suffering, in earthly life, is not based on the degree of guilt. Suffering is not a punishment from a vengeful God, but a conditioning process. Our inner selves must transcend the natural, human way of thinking, acting, relating, and responding, and attune ourselves to God's way. To live the God-life it is necessary to become like God, just as the child must spiritually, psychologically, and physically become "adult" in order to meaningfully participate in an adult world. When adults look back on their formative years, they may remember many unpleasant experiences, but they also admit that they learned valuable lessons they could not have understood any other way.

The soul's growth in God will consist of both joyful and painful experiences, as does the child's growth into adulthood. Children, in their limited wisdom, view with distaste many of the things that their parents insist upon — nutritious meals, proper rest, cleanliness, medical and dental treatment, going to school and to church, etc. — but as the child gains wisdom and insight, he chooses these very same things for himself. With greater wisdom he begins to see the whole picture, not just the present moment and instant gratification.

Most people begin receiving religious instruction during their childhood. It is received in segments, like the pieces of a jigsaw puzzle. Since children take things literally, they often form a mental image of spiritual matters that is far from being accurate. As the pieces are fitted together through the years, the picture may become more and more distorted as new pieces are continually added.

God, the Father, was often pictured as old, with a long,

white beard. People who "went to heaven" were thought of as "up in the sky floating on clouds," usually "playing harps." For many people, this picture of heaven was boring and completely unappealing. God was often perceived, through human projection, as a stern, judgmental disciplinarian, waiting — even eager — to strike the hapless individual who got out of line. The purification or conditioning process, purgatory, was believed to be like a jail, where one served time, and was eventually let out on good behavior. Saints were frequently considered solemn individuals who usually never had any fun, rejected the world and its beauty, and stifled most of their God-given human instincts, rather like walking statues. Other children pictured Saints as people with extraordinary powers, a little like Wonder Woman or Superman.

On the other hand, hell was usually pictured as filled with well-meaning, likeable people who had somehow made a few mistakes. Young people often jokingly said that, since most of their friends would be in hell, they would just as soon go there. It was generally understood that all of the fun things that religion frowned upon would be permissible, and that it resembled a wild, ongoing drunken revel.

Between the Puritan influence, and the tendency to project a human way of thinking upon God, Christian faith often seemed just about impossible to live and, if it was lived, would be tedious and dismal. It is no wonder that this version of Christianity was rejected by so many. It wasn't that true faith was abandoned or rejected, for it was never clearly understood. When the false images formed in childhood were examined with adult wisdom, they often seemed unacceptable. This is how it should be, but a re-learning on an adult level is necessary. The pieces of the puzzle can be separated, then rearranged to form a clear picture, and none of the true beliefs need be lost. It is only the false images and misconceptions that we are advised to give up.

Heaven, hell, and purgatory are not places, but states of being, like being in love. Purgatory is the purifying process necessary before the soul can be raised to a supernatural level, and on earth it includes the desert and the dark nights. The divine love relationship, which readies the soul for heaven, has to begin on earth. The soul that God leads into the desert can rejoice, for it is being prepared for divine intimacy.

"Christianity is not, as it is sometimes presented and sometimes practised, an additional burden of observances and obligations to weigh down and increase the already heavy load, or to multiply the already paralysing ties of our life in society. It is, in fact, a SOUL OF IMMENSE POWER WHICH BESTOWS SIGNIFICANCE AND BEAUTY AND A NEW LIGHTNESS ON WHAT WE ARE ALREADY DOING" *(Divine Milieu,* Teilhard de Chardin, p. 70).

Just as physical development proceeds through infancy, childhood, adolescence, adulthood, and old age, spiritual development goes through definite, though not always apparent, stages of growth.

The Three Stages of Human Existence

WOMB	EARTHLY LIFE	ETERNAL LIFE
Conception: Fusion of Divine Spirit and human spirit. United with God but unaware, infant develops until it is able to exist on earth. Unknowingly, and with no effort, shares in mother's life. Birth will necessitate existence in an entirely new dimension.	Conscious awareness begins, and ability to receive and return human love. Spiritual awareness begins, and ability to receive and return Divine Love. Soul is conditioned and strengthened through love, prayer, suffering, and practice of virtues, in preparation for becoming LIKE God. Through spiritual growth, begins to enjoy foretaste of union with God as in heavenly existence.	Birth into eternal life again necessitates existence in an unknown dimension, formerly inconceivable to human mind. Through growth in Agape Love the soul has been brought to fullness of its divine potential, now able to share the God-life in knowledgeable participation. The soul is exalted, divinized, and through Union, Divine Transformation, and Spiritual Marriage is made the "equal" of Christ, sharing in Trinitarian life, with its love, joy, and peace for all eternity.

The soul comes forth from God . . . and returns to God (in this respect, a circle is more accurate). The divine life, like a golden thread, runs throughout our entire existence.

There is one continuous existence, but in three distinct and entirely different stages. Just as earthly life is incomprehensible to an infant still in the womb, heavenly existence is impossible for those still in their earthly life to accurately picture or describe. Through a gradual process, the human spirit is slowly conditioned to bear the full weight of God's glory, to be clothed in His divinity, and to breathe the Spirit of Love in unison with the Father and the Son.

"One should not think it impossible that the soul be capable of so sublime an activity as this breathing in God, through participation as God breathes in her. . . . This is transformation in the three Persons in power and wisdom and love, and thus the soul is like God through this transformation. HE CREATED HER IN HIS IMAGE AND LIKENESS THAT SHE MIGHT ATTAIN SUCH RESEMBLANCE" (Spiritual Canticle, St. John of the Cross, St. 39:4).

To take the second stage of human existence, earthly life, out of context and consider it the beginning and end of human existence is to cut us off from both our divine roots and our glorious destiny. This frame of mind renders spiritual growth principles meaningless, makes life often seem empty, and death something to fear. It gives rise to the attitude of "grabbing all that you can get before it is over," which leads to still further anxiety and frustration, for mankind intuitively senses that it was created for something MAGNIFICENT. The fact that much of mankind has not found it yet sends these people in endless pursuit of further distractions and escapes. Peace of mind comes only in knowing who we are, why we are here, and where we are headed.

"My dear people, we are already the children of God

but what we are to be in the future has not yet been revealed; all we know is, that when it is revealed WE SHALL BE LIKE HIM" (1 John 3:2).

"Even in this world we have become as He is" (1 John 4:17).

Growth and change can be painful, but unbelievably enriching. To be raised from a human level to the Divine is a transformation process that requires time, effort, and cooperation. Whatever the events of our lives or how we feel about them, we are steadily moving closer toward our goal of union with God. Nothing is lost, the good and the bad, the large and the small happenings, for God makes use of everything for His one purpose of preparing the soul for divine life by raising it to His level, and making the soul His equal. Love finds equals, or makes equals.

"For the property of love is to make the lover equal to the object loved. Since the soul in this state possesses perfect love, she is called the bride of the Son of God, which signifies equality with Him. In this equality of friendship the possessions of both are held in common" (*Spiritual Canticle*, St. John of the Cross, 28:1).

Whatever the degree of progress during our earthly lives, the divine fullness will only be realized in its perfection as a permanent state in eternal life. The bride/soul is aware of being transformed in God, but the uninterrupted enjoyment of that state must wait for heaven.

"He is usually there, in this embrace with His bride, as though asleep in the substance of the soul. And it is very well aware of Him and ordinarily enjoys Him. Were He always awake within it, communicating knowledge and love, it would already be in glory" (*Living Flame of Love*, St. John of the Cross, St. 4:15).

Some people may equate their spiritual condition and degree of progress with feelings of being close to God, a sense of peace, and enjoying days in which everything runs smoothly. Life itself is not always like that. Everything is a part of growth. The spiritual journey is not so much a straight, smooth road, as an undulating path, or an "alternating current" with its ups and downs, but always moving forward.

If we pictured earthly life as a graph, it might look something like this:

ENJOYABLE EXPERIENCES

Natural: Human love, marriage or other vocation, family, friends, creative activity, work, enjoyment of simplicity of life and beauty of creation.

Spiritual: Sense of God's presence, "oasis" times in prayer, "touches" or "wounds" of love, experiencing Union, Spiritual Marriage.

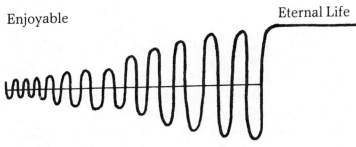

Enjoyable

Eternal Life

Painful

PAINFUL EXPERIENCES

Natural: Illness, loss of loved one, poverty, loneliness, misunderstanding with family or friend, disappointments, setback in career, etc.

Spiritual: "Desert" times, aridity in prayer, "dark night" experiences, the emptying or stripping of the soul.

Frequently, the natural and spiritual will be experienced together and intensify each other. The joyful becomes more delightful, the painful seems more severe. Through these ups and downs, human will becomes synchronized with Divine Will and, eventually, the soul and God are vibrating on the same wavelength and in complete harmony.

All joy and all suffering, whether physical, psychological, or spiritual, serves to expand the soul's capacity for love and to ready it for divine transformation. Anything in human nature that is contrary to Union with God will be eliminated. All that is good in human nature will be purified, strengthened, and exalted, raised from the natural plane to the supernatural plane. "Anyone who is joined to the Lord is one Spirit with Him" (1 Corinthians 6:17).

The world of nature consists of day and night, sun and rain, summer and winter. The ups and downs of life are all part of spiritual development, cleansing the soul of impediments to Union. This process has been compared to a diamond cutter working to bring out the facets of a stone to catch and reflect the light, or a sculptor chipping away at a block of marble to form a beautiful statue. It is said that even the flaws of the stone are used to enhance the end results under skillful, loving hands. Michaelangelo, when asked how he sculpted his magnificent statue of David, replied: "I just chipped away all that was not David." In order for the soul to become divine, God chips away all that is not divine.

The paradox of the spiritual life is such that "desert" or "dark night" experiences are both enriching and diminishing. Unlike the natural world, where complete emptying is necessary before filling, in the spiritual area there is a constant "back and forth" dynamic. Throughout the spiritual journey there is an emptying and filling, a seeking and finding, or a stripping and clothing of the soul.

During times of suffering, illness, or loss, the "eyes of the soul" suddenly begin to "see," as if adjusting an out-of-focus lens, and the soul may receive its first clear glimpse of spiritual realities. When the soul, as described in the Old

Testament, is "brought low," or has its "mouth placed in the dust," then the things of this world may be seen in their true light, as temporary and passing. Earthly goals or possessions that once seemed to be of the highest priority are more easily placed in perspective. The "prizes" of the worldly suddenly seem to be no more than children's toys, with the realization that people are more important than "things."

Experiences such as these have been dramatic turning points (metanoia) in the lives of some of the Saints. St. Francis of Assisi was a wealthy playboy living mainly for pleasure, until he was brought close to death through illness. Upon recovery, Francis embraced poverty and founded the Franciscan Order, from then on living the Love of God expressed not just in words, but by serving his brothers and sisters. St. Ignatius Loyola was prepared for a brilliant career in the army until he was wounded in the leg. During the forced inactivity of his convalescence, Ignatius discerned that God was leading him in a different direction, and he founded the Society of Jesus, the "Jesuits." St. Paul, on the way to Damascus, was "thrown from his high horse," his misguided attempt to exterminate Christians and, instead, joined the Apostles in spreading the Christian message.

When, because of Lent, a retreat, or a commitment to prayer, we temporarily put aside our worldly preoccupations for spiritual reasons, we discover that we travel lighter, are able to get along with less, and find it easier to give our undivided attention to God. It is for these reasons that most religions have emphasized regular times for penance and fasting, or temporarily denying the body for the sake of the soul. The hunger of the body is usually attended to; the hunger of the spirit may not receive the proper nourishment. In simplicity of life, and times of silence, the gentle stirrings of love are more easily sensed and responded to by the soul.

The heightened intuitive awareness attained through

love, prayer, or suffering is a preparation for the "Promised Land" not only in eternity, but our experiential encounter with the Indwelling God here and now. "The soul feels Him within itself not only as a fire which has consumed and transformed it, but as a fire that burns and flares within it, as I mentioned. And that flame, every time it flares up, bathes the soul in glory and refreshes it with the quality of divine life. Such is the activity of the Holy Spirit in the soul transformed in love" (*Living Flame of Love*, St. John of the Cross, St. 1:3).

The only difference between the spiritual journey of the Saints and that of the majority of souls is that, in order to be brought to the fullness of divine transformation in a shorter length of time, the Saints' experiences were necessarily more extreme and intensified. The spiritual graph of a Saint would show higher peaks, deeper valleys, and a shorter time span. Their enjoyment of God was, at times, more delightful or ecstatic, but a more radical emptying of the soul and more painful purification process was necessary to accommodate the massive infusions of divine life.

"The union wrought between the two natures and the communication of the divine to the human in this state is such that even though neither change their being, both appear to be God" (*Spiritual Canticle*, St. John of the Cross, ch. 22:4).

Sanctity is a state of "be"-ing, not "do"-ing, although good works will automatically flow from a soul in this state as from the heart of God Himself, for the soul and God are now one. "This is the reason for prayer, my daughters, the purpose of this spiritual marriage: the birth always of good works, good works" (*Interior Castle*, St. Teresa of Avila, VII:4, 6). We are not always called to imitate the outward way of life of the Saints, but their interior way, the soul's growth into what it was meant to be — like God — is their message.

Although the Saints have often been pictured as Wonder

Woman or Superman, who have performed fantastic deeds far beyond human capacity, it is important to realize that what is admired as their strengths is the power of God working through them as instruments. We see them after they have become divinized, the way that we will all be in time, for everyone is called to become a saint.

We may not all be Saints, with a capital "S" (canonized), but saints nevertheless, for the end result will be the same as each soul reaches its fullest potential. God alone can make "Saints." When the Church, after thorough investigation, believes there is sufficient proof that God has brought an individual to the highest stage of divine transformation possible in this life, he or she is "canonized," and approved as a role model and teacher for others.

Since to be "in heaven" means to be transformed in God, there are billions of saints, all the loving, faithful parents, grandparents, spouses, sisters, brothers, or other relatives and friends, unknown except to their loved ones. In their blissful state of sharing the divine life it is doubtful that they would be bothered about their earthly status and whether or not they are "canonized," but all of the saints are concerned for us as younger brothers and sisters.

For inspiration and guidance it is not necessary to choose "either" Scripture "or" the Saints. There is no discrepancy between the teachings of the Gospel and the teachings and examples of the Saints. The Saints lived the Gospel message. They were ordinary human beings, witnessing with their lives the truth and power of the promises of Christ. There is one Spirit of Christ, but each person is unique. The Spirit of Christ is lived in many ways, according to the spiritual path, the individual personality, state of life, culture, and the times. The lives of the Saints are, therefore, a source of hope and encouragement for everyone for they started out, just like the rest of us, as weak human beings. "They were weak people who were given strength" (Hebrews 11:35). Saints are the "divine successes" referred to by Chardin.

History repeats itself, and human nature is still the same. The Saints did not start life as perfect human beings, and neither do we. At different stages in our lives, we are able to see ourselves as sinners like Dismas or Mary Magdalene, doubters like Thomas, denying Christ as Peter did, and fearful and weak like the other Apostles. But we are also the strengthened, Spirit-led Apostles, the repentant, reformed sinners like the Magdalene, as we sit at the Master's feet gazing in loving contemplation. Or like Dismas who, in one perfect act of agape love which touched the heart of Jesus, made up for a lifetime of crime, was restored to inner wholeness, and promised Paradise. Spiritually, we agonize with Jesus in the Garden, fall many times beneath our burdens, and die to our former selves, to be united with Him in love. Through this transforming union, we are brought to the fullness of life and our divine potential — the joy and power of the Resurrection!

In John 15:13, Jesus said, "A man can have no greater love than to lay down his life for his friends." A life can be given up by putting aside one's own inclinations or desires in response to God's call, a giving up of a good for the sake of a higher good, such as through a "religious vocation." There are also ways to "lay down a life" a drop at a time, through the days, months, and years of loving faithfulness to duty of the ordinary life in the world, in the face of what has been described as the "heroism of the ordinary," or the "monotony of the everyday," which is the way to sanctity for most of the children of God, called to be saints of the ordinary. Sanctity was never meant to be so complicated or difficult that it was beyond the attainment of the average person. "It is never the will of your Father in heaven that one of these little ones should be lost" (Matthew 18:14).

Awareness of the soul's journey begins when it is "born again" and begins to "see" and "know" throughout its spiritual childhood, similar to the way that the newborn infant's senses and faculties develop and mature. Guided by the inner light of its love relationship with the Lord, the soul is led through purification (purgatory); illumination (enlightenment and growth in divine wisdom); union (oneness of wills achieved through the surrender of the lower/human, to the higher/divine, another giving up of a good for the sake of a higher good); and divine transform-mation or spiritual marriage (heaven) as, overwhelmed and inflamed with love, the soul is lifted (exalted, glorified) into the embrace of the Trinity.

The exaltation of the soul is implicit in the belief in the Assumption of Mary, and the levitations, raptures, and ecstasies ("going out of oneself, transcending the natural") of some of the Saints. These mystical phenomena, which many people associate with sanctity, are the outward manifestations of God's activity in the soul in a more in-tense way. Teresa of Avila had numerous mystical ex-periences in the early and middle stages of her spiritual journey, but the raptures ended when she received the grace of spiritual marriage. Teresa attributed her former experiences to her "weakness." The spiritually unpre-pared soul, not yet God's equal, is unable to withstand the power of the divine inflow.

Many spiritual writers, including Teresa, remind their readers that it is not the externals that are important, but what is taking place in the soul. They advise against seek-ing raptures and such, for souls could deceive themselves into imagining the experience, and do themselves much harm. Teresa and John of the Cross insist on love, humil-ity/truth which ensures self-knowledge, prayer, practicing the virtues, faithfulness and determination as the tried and true way; for God's methods most often accomplish the desired end in a hidden manner. Eventually, through discerning and following God's will, every soul will "tran-scend the natural."

"Since His words are effected in us as deeds, they must have worked in such a manner in those souls already dis-posed that everything corporeal in the soul was taken away and it was left pure spirit. Thus the soul could be joined in this heavenly union with the uncreated Spirit. For it is very certain that in emptying ourselves of all that is creature and detaching ourselves from it for the love of God, the same Lord will fill us with Himself. . . . I don't know what greater love there can be than this. And ALL OF US ARE INCLUDED HERE, for His Majesty said: 'I ask not only for them but for all those who also will believe in Me'; and He says: 'I am in them' '' (Interior Castle, St. Teresa of Avila, VII:2, 7).

"Once being asked how one becomes enraptured, the Venerable Father John of the Cross replied: 'by denying one's own will and doing the will of God; for an ecstasy is nothing else than going out of self and being caught up in God; and this is what he who obeys does; he leaves himself and his desire, and thus unburdened plunges himself in God' '' (Maxims on Love, St. John of the Cross, 80).

When God does make use of visible manifestations, such as raptures, ecstasies, and being "lifted up," these experiences present a vivid picture of indescribable heavenly bliss, exaltation, the yet-to-be-seen destiny of every soul, and are often a means of renewing humanity's lagging faith. This living witness is a reminder that the same spiritual development proceeds in other souls, although gradually and without unusual occurrences. To read about the experiences of the Saints who endured suffering, doubts, and uncertainty, but with determined love have reached their goal, gives renewed hope and inspiration to others.

The joyful experiences of the soul's progress are welcomed by most people, but this "filling" can only be achieved after a corresponding "emptying." The sense of the "absence of God" that everyone experiences at one time or other is actually a positive step, a sign of spiritual growth. It not only reveals that divine love has been growing in the soul, but that the soul's inner awareness has recognized and absorbed that love. If a stranger passed by on the street and was never seen again, it would cause no concern. If a dear loved one went away, even for a little while, there would be a deep longing and sense of absence, a fragmenting of the spirit, for the individual would have been accustomed to the nearness and oneness of love, and is aware of the cause of the longing.

The soul's longings and hungers are not always recognized for what they are. This "absence of God" and corresponding yearning of the soul is often referred to as a "desert experience," because of the feelings of aridity, barrenness, and emptiness, where there had once been love, joy, and delight in the Lord and in prayer. Experiencing what they believe is God's "absence," many people mistakenly think that they have "lost" God through some fault of their own. This can be the beginning of a "dark night," for the soul that begins to sense its emptiness must proceed in faith, which is obscure to the created intellect. In his various writings, John of the Cross touches on all of these problems that usually occur during the spiritual journey.

"If there is no one to understand these persons, they either turn back and abandon the road or lose courage. . . . They fatigue and overwork themselves, thinking that they are failing because of their negligences or sins. . . . Those who are in this situation should feel comforted; they ought to persevere patiently and not be afflicted. Let them trust in God Who does not fail those who seek Him with a simple and righteous heart" (Dark Night, St. John of the Cross, Bk. I, ch. 10:2, 3).

"For it is through the delight and satisfaction they experienced in prayer that they have become detached from worldly things and have gained some spiritual strength in God." And through this strength, John says, "they will be able to suffer a little oppression and dryness without turning back. . . . He leaves them in such dryness that they not only fail to receive satisfaction and pleasure from their spiritual exercises and works, as they formerly did, but also find these exercises distasteful and bitter. As I said, when God sees that they have grown a little, He weans them from the sweet breast so that they might be strengthened, lays aside their swaddling bands, and puts them down from His arms that they may grow accustomed to walking by themselves. This change is a surprise to them because everything seems to be functioning in reverse" (Ibid., ch. 8:3).

"The soul must first be set in emptiness and poverty of spirit and purged of every natural support, consolation, and apprehension, earthly and heavenly. Thus empty, it is truly poor in spirit and stripped of the old man, and thereby able to live that new and blessed life which is the state of union with God, attained by means of this night" (Ibid., ch. 9:4).

The spiritual desert is the borderline between the natural, which is under our control, and the supernatural, where the spiritual child must be led by God. Many people turn back at this point, mistakenly believing that contemplation is not for them. Some people proceed to throw themselves into various causes and movements, and insist that "work is prayer." This statement is a partial truth. Everything is prayer when the soul has an inner relationship with God and is following His will, for then all of the daily routine becomes sanctified.

The love and delight of the earlier prayer relationship is meant to strengthen and fortify the soul so that it will not run from these inner stirrings but endure the desert journey. A desert place is where we leave all non-essentials behind and spend time in silence and solitude with our Divine Friend within. All love relationships, if they are to grow, need time devoted entirely to each other.

"That is why I am going to lure her. I will allure her. I will lead her into the desert and speak to her heart. . . . I will make a covenant. I will espouse you in fidelity and you shall know [experience] the Lord" (Hosea 2:16).

The painful emotional state of adolescence could be compared to the desert experience. The adolescent, going through a transition in preparation for adulthood, becomes extremely sensitive. The adolescent has not reached full potential or self-individuation, is often still "searching for identity," and has little confidence. There is almost a "stripping" of the emotional/psychological areas, a coming out of the protective childhood shell. Childhood ways are left behind, and the adult person is not yet fully formed, causing a sense of one's vulnerability or defenselessness in this in-between state. At this stage it is a great help to have understanding people to talk to. Physical activity, good nutrition and proper rest make good sense, and enjoying one's friends and a sense of humor are indispensable.

Because of the exposed feelings of the adolescent, little things that may seem trivial to adults often seem unbelievably wonderful ("cloud nine"), or exaggeratedly painful ("in the pits"), to the young. There is one process of physical development, but it is experienced uniquely by each young person, depending a great deal upon their personality and temperament. Because everyone takes adolescence for granted as part of normal development, most adolescents are not overly upset by it, and manage to survive and grow into healthy adults.

Just as to reach adulthood one has to go through adolescence, to reach the "Promised Land" the desert must be traversed. It would be a mistake for a soul to turn back at this point. The desert experience is painful because the soul is being stripped of the old ways in preparation for spiritual maturity and union with God. Like the adolescent, the soul has not yet reached its full potential nor realized its spiritual identity. This "spiritual adolescence" is not as well known, and often comes as a surprise to the prayerful soul.

"The soul, then, should advert that God is the principal agent in this matter, and that He acts as the blind man's guide who must lead it by the hand to the place it does not know how to reach (to supernatural things of which neither its intellect, will, nor memory can know the nature)'' (*Living Flame of Love*, St. John of the Cross, St. 3:29).

In this spiritual state, it is also a great help to have friends to laugh with and talk to, for affirmation, encouragement, and prayerful support. The elements of a balanced life previously suggested, especially a sense of humor, could be considered necessities in the "desert." Desert experiences are times of significant growth for the soul remains faithful only out of its love for God (agape), and not because it enjoys spiritual consolations. Love must often be lived under adverse conditions, to expand its capacity to that of the divine.

In the Carmelite tradition, the desert experience is an essential part of growth in self-knowledge. Teresa states that the Lord leads souls into the desert "in order to try His lovers and know whether they will be able to drink the chalice and help Him carry the cross before He lays great treasures within them. . . . The favors that come afterward are of such great worth that He desires first that before He gives them to us we see by experience our own worthlessness" (*Ibid.*, ch. 11:11).

Feelings "about" God are not God, and the soul determined to follow the contemplative path will settle for nothing less than union with God. It is easy to be faithful to the spiritual life when prayer is delightful, and things are going well. When we reach the desert and God seems far away, or in the dark night as doubts assail us, these are opportune times for calling forth a stronger faith-response, just as in weight lifting the muscles must meet with ever-increasing resistance in order to continue developing. The spiritual life is dynamic and ever-changing, and if we are not progressing we are sliding backward.

"Conformity with God's will must be the goal of one's strivings. To persevere in prayer and the struggle involved is to go forward" (*Interior Castle*, St. Teresa of Avila, Introduction).

If a man was told that he was eligible for a vast inheritance, but that he would have to travel to a different country and, along the way, learn how to manage the estates and holdings in the manner of his wealthy benefactor, he would probably not have a moment's hesitation. Any type of travel accommodations would be eagerly accepted. The hardships, illnesses, or setbacks of the journey would be patiently endured, with the thought ever in mind of what awaited him at the journey's end. It is unlikely that he would give up the goal and decide to settle down at some point along the way, no matter how enjoyable. Nor would he turn back at the first obstacle, and he would probably be willing to undergo any necessary testing or trials.

Effort, willingness to change, and even pain are taken for granted and endured for many of the world's temporary goals: physical fitness, sports, career advancement, etc. Time and effort are expended in deciding where to spend a vacation. Some people plan and work for a lifetime toward retirement which, at best, usually amounts to a few years. And yet, never-ending, eternal life often may not get so much as a passing thought.

Many people, even in something as important as their faith, are content with the superficial. They skim the surface, and their spiritual life remains shallow. Our souls are meant to be clear, limpid pools, the greater the depth and stillness, the clearer and more vivid the divine reflection. For this, an emptying or hollowing out is required. The depths are only attained at the cost of some time, effort, and suffering. As in other areas of life, love makes it endurable.

The "key to the kingdom" through the "narrow gate" is the way marked out by Jesus and followed by Christians through the centuries, the way of the Cross. The self-willed, self-centered, natural man, who lives by instinct alone, must die in order to move into a higher level of existence and "put on Christ."

"You have stripped off your old behavior with your old

self, and you have put on a new self which will progress towards true knowledge the more it is renewed in the image of its creator" (Colossians 3:9).

"For the rest of his life on earth he is not ruled by human passions but only by the will of God" (1 Peter 4:2).

The world is amazed at the splendor and vastness of outer space, yet within each person there exists a greater infinity, the Abyss of Divinity, the unseen Creator of all that we see and admire. As one must have extensive training and preparation in order to journey into outer space, some preparation is necessary for the journey into inner space. In regular contemplative prayer we "train" our scattered thoughts and wayward affections, like unruly children, to behave. We prepare ourselves by "exercising" our virtues every day, and by spiritual reading. We accept the fact that the natural laws of time and gravity do not operate in outer space the same way that they do on earth, and should not be surprised that in the world of the spirit they do not exist at all. Just as everything must be germ free before a space trip, in our inner depths the Fire of Love must purify the soul in preparation for spiritual marriage.

An ever-deepening union in love, and the awareness and enjoyment of that union, is God's plan for each soul. "Oh, come to the water all you who are thirsty. . . . Pay attention, come to Me: listen, and your soul will live. . . . With you I will make an everlasting covenant" (Isaiah 55:1, 3).

The thirsting of the soul in its "desert journey" brings an ever-growing longing for the "oasis" and "rest." Water is a matter of life or death, and is especially symbolic in parts of the world where desert lands are numerous. Water has been used in Scripture and spiritual writings to symbolize both the Holy Spirit and the infusion of the Spirit in the "waters of contemplation."

"Once more there will be poured on us the spirit from above. . . . Water gushes in the desert, streams in the wasteland, the scorched earth becomes a lake, the parched land [soul] springs of water" (Isaiah 32:15, 35:7).

"The water that I shall give will turn into a spring inside him, welling up to eternal life" (John 4:14).

The Scripture story of the Samaritan woman at the well was a favorite of St. Teresa of Avila, who used the various ways of obtaining water to explain the progressive stages of prayer. Teresa wrote many explanations and frequent words of encouragement for beginners, confident that if more souls understood the way God works in the soul, they would not turn back or abandon contemplative prayer.

"It seems to me the garden [soul] can be watered in four ways. You may draw water from a well (which is for us a lot of work). Or you may get it by means of a water wheel and aqueducts in such a way that it is obtained by turning the crank of the water wheel. (I have drawn it this way sometimes — the method involves less work than the other, and you get more water.) Or it may flow from a river or a stream. (The garden is watered much better by this means because the ground is more fully soaked, and there is no need to water so frequently — and much less work for the gardener.) Or the water may be provided by a great deal of rain. (For the Lord waters the garden without any work on our part — and this way is incomparably better than all the others mentioned)" (Life, St. Teresa, ch. 11:7).

Newcomers to contemplative prayer usually begin with discursive meditation and acquired contemplation or the prayer of recollection, all of which require some preparation and initial effort.

"Beginners in prayer, we can say, are those who draw water from the well. This involves a lot of work on their own part, as I have said. They must tire themselves in trying to recollect their senses. Since they are accustomed to being distracted, this recollection requires much effort. . . . This discursive work with the intellect is what is meant by fetching water from the well. . . . The Master has confidence in the gardener because He sees that without any pay [consolations] he is so very careful about what he was told to do. This gardener helps Christ carry the cross and reflects that the Lord lived with it all during his life. . . . And so he is determined, even though this dryness may last for his whole life, not to let Christ fall with the cross. The time will come when the Lord will repay him all at once. He doesn't fear that the labor is being wasted. He is serving a good Master whose eyes are upon him" (Life, St. Teresa of Avila, ch. 11:7, 9-10).

Intention and attitude are all-important. Teresa states that the soul with determination who remains faithful in aridity "has travelled a great part of the way," and is assured of "a solid foundation" (Ibid., ch. 11:13).

Whether the soul is a beginner, or at the highest stages of prayer, the journey still has its joyful and painful experiences. "The greatest labor is in the beginning because it is the beginner who works while the Lord gives the increase. In the other degrees of prayer the greatest thing is enjoying; although whether in the beginning, the middle, or the end, all bear their crosses even though these crosses be different" (Ibid., 11:5).

"There are many who begin, yet they never reach the end. I believe this is due mainly to a failure to embrace the cross from the beginning; thinking they are doing nothing, they become afflicted. When the intellect ceases to work, they cannot bear it. But it is then perhaps that their will is being strengthened and fortified, although they may not be aware of this" (Ibid., ch. 11:15).

"If the intellect is not active, the soul is left very dry, like a desert. Since this edifice is built entirely on humility, the closer one comes to God the more progress there must be in this virtue; and if there is no progress in humility, everything is going to be ruined" (Ibid., ch. 12:4).

The path of prayer is far from being rigid and legalistic. "Now strive in the beginning to walk in joy and freedom, for there are some persons who think their devotion will go away if they become a little distracted" (*Ibid.*, ch. 13:1).

Teresa assures souls, "Have great confidence, for it is necessary not to hold back one's desires, but to BELIEVE IN GOD THAT IF WE TRY WE SHALL LITTLE BY LITTLE, EVEN THOUGH IT MAY NOT BE SOON, REACH THE STATE THE SAINTS DID WITH HIS HELP . . ." (*Ibid.*, ch. 13:2).

Infused contemplation begins with the second way, the water wheel and aqueducts; Teresa calls this "the prayer of quiet," which is "something supernatural because in no way can it [soul] acquire this prayer through any efforts it may make" (*Ibid.*, ch. 14:1-2).

Teresa's description of what the soul experiences emphasizes the necessity of the gradual surrendering of the will. "In this prayer the faculties are gathered within so as to enjoy that satisfaction with greater delight. But they are not lost, nor do they sleep. Only the will [love] is occupied in such a way that, without knowing how, it becomes captive: it merely consents to God allowing Him to imprison it as one who well knows how to be the captive of its Lover" (*Ibid.*, ch. 14:2).

"This water I believe makes the virtues grow better and also brings the soul much closer to the true Virtue, which is God, from whence come all the virtues. His Majesty is beginning to communicate Himself to this soul, and He wants it to experience how He is doing so" (*Ibid.*, ch. 14:5).

Because Teresa had once abandoned prayer, she is careful to warn others so that they will not make the same mistake. "I should like to explain this experience because we are dealing with beginners; and when the Lord begins to grant these favors, the soul itself doesn't understand them nor does it know what to do with itself. For if the Lord leads it along the path of fear, as He did me, it is a great trial if there is no one to understand it. To see itself described brings it intense joy, and then it sees clearly the path it is walking on. It is a great good to know what one must do in order to advance in any of these stages. For I have suffered much and have lost a great deal of time for not knowing what to do, and I pity souls greatly who find themselves alone when they arrive at this stage" (Ibid., ch. 14:7).

The "third water," "flowing from a river or spring," Teresa describes as "a sleep of the faculties." "This prayer is a glorious foolishness, a heavenly madness where the true wisdom is learned: and it is for the soul a most delightful way of enjoying" (Ibid., ch. 16:1).

"God's foolishness is wiser than human wisdom" (1 Corinthians 1:25).

"The Lord often gave me this prayer in abundance, and I didn't understand it: nor did I know how to speak of it. . . . I did understand clearly that it was not a complete union of all the faculties and that this type of prayer was more excellent than the previous one . . . the faculties are almost totally united with God but not so absorbed as not to function . . . the flowers [virtues] are blossoming. . . . Here I think it is advisable . . . to abandon oneself completely into the hands of God" (Life, St. Teresa of Avila, ch. 16:2-3; ch. 17:1).

The "fourth water" is how Teresa symbolized the prayer of union. She was concerned about her ability to clearly describe this high stage of prayer.

"But I believe the Lord will help me in this explanation. His Majesty knows that besides obeying it is my intention to attract souls to so high a blessing. . . . God enlightened my intellect: sometimes with words, at other times showing me how to explain this favor, as He did with the previous prayer. His Majesty, it seems, wanted to say what I neither was able nor knew how to say" (Ibid., ch. 18:8).

"In this fourth water the soul isn't in possession of its senses, but it rejoices without understanding what it is rejoicing in. It understands that it is enjoying a good in which are gathered together all goods, but this good is incomprehensible. All the senses are occupied in this joy. . . . How this prayer they call union comes about and what it is, I don't know how to explain. . . . What union is we already know since it means that two separate things become one. . . . The elevation of the spirit, or joining with heavenly love, takes place within this very union" *(Ibid.,* ch. 18:1-3, 7).

"The soul is much more improved and in a higher state than it was after the previous degrees of prayer. Its humility is deeper because it sees plainly that through no diligence of its own did it receive that very generous and magnificent gift and that it played no role in obtaining or experiencing it" *(Ibid.,* ch. 19:2).

This uniting of the soul and its faculties with God is the result of the desert and dark night experiences, where faith, hope, and love are tested and fortified. "Don't think even though it may seem so to you, that virtue has already been gained if it hasn't been tried by its contrary" *(Ibid.,* ch. 31:19).

The Saints were the spiritual explorers or time travelers who, through the vehicle of God's grace, moved in spirit through time and into eternity, then returned to chart spiritual directions for all of those who were to journey after them. Just like our earthly travels, no two trips will be the same. The road and landmarks will be the same, but the journey will be uniquely experienced by each individual. Every soul has to "cross the desert" and "climb the mountain," but they are reassured by the Saints, who have been there, the "Promised Land" is a reality, and that the soul's efforts and determination to continue, in spite of aridity, will not be in vain.

"A person must always take care so that when one kind of water is lacking he might strive for the other. This water from heaven often comes when the gardener is least expecting it. True, in the beginning it almost always occurs after a long period of mental prayer. . . . What a tremendous reward; one moment is enough to repay all the trials that can be suffered in life!" *(Ibid.,* ch. 18:9).

"Those who by such a method can enclose themselves

within this little heaven of our soul, where the Maker of heaven and earth is present, and grow accustomed to refusing to be where the exterior senses in their distraction have gone or look in that direction should believe they are following an excellent path and that they will not fail to drink water from the fount: for they will journey far in a short time. . . . Drinking from it is perfect contemplation'' (Way of Perfection, St. Teresa of Avila, ch. 28:5; 32:9).

"Then let all who are thirsty come: all who want it may have the water of life, and have it free" (Revelation 22:17).

The water of the Spirit seeps in through the least opening, adapts itself to any level, and assumes the form of every vessel. The vessel itself then becomes an "oasis" or well, a carrier and a fountain of living water for other thirsty souls. Each soul drinks according to its thirst, and is filled according to its capacity.

"If any man is thirsty, let him come to Me! Let the man come and drink who believes in Me! As scripture says: From his breast shall flow fountains of living water" (John 7:37).

6

Approaches to Contemplative Prayer

Any one of the many approaches to contemplative prayer, from various traditions, can be helpful depending upon the disposition and temperament of the particular individual, and the path on which God is leading the soul. One "road" is not necessarily better than another when they all lead to the same place. It is the soul's relationship with the Indwelling God that is important, not how the soul arrived at that relationship.

Some spiritual principles will always be effective, and realizing the continuity of these traditions encourages the soul to rest in the timeless power of God. One of the most ancient learning methods of contemplative prayer is the "master/disciple" relationship, frequently depicted in the Old Testament, in which the prophet or holyman passed the spiritual torch of his own inner light to his disciple. The disciple, searching for a deeper relationship with his God, would stay with the renowned master, absorbing not only his way of prayer but his way of life, his spirit and virtues, communicated not solely with words but through the master's very "be"-ing, witnessed in the simplicity of daily existence (spiritual osmosis).

The spiritual preparation of the disciple was a prerequisite for growth in inner light. The disciple did not seek divine wisdom solely for his own benefit, but as a means of helping and guiding his people. The same apostolic dimension exists today, in an even broader scope. God still comes "through" individuals, not just "to" them, and there is a need for willing, spiritually committed souls as "channels," "messengers," "witnesses," "lamps," or "carriers" of God's love and light to a world sorely in need, a "spiritual priesthood" which is ordained by God.

All men and women are called to participate, in varying degrees, in this ministry of "spiritual priesthood" and are meant to be "living Eucharists," aiding and encouraging one another's spiritual growth. This inner transmission of Spirit, prompted by God from the soul's depths, is accomplished by reflecting our unique Divine Image to one another.

"And we, with our unveiled faces reflecting like mirrors the brightness of the Lord [Shekinah], all grow brighter and brighter as we are turned into the image that we reflect. [The contemplation of God in Christ gives the Christian a likeness to God]" (2 Corinthians 3:18g).

The soul committed to God automatically "consecrates" everything to God by an inner dedication. "Consecrate: con — thoroughly + sacrare — to treat as sacred, make holy." As the priest takes ordinary bread and, through his inner commitment and intention of being the instrument through which God works, raises the ordinary to the level of the Divine, each individual, through the spiritual priesthood ordained by God, sanctifies or "lifts up" to God the minutes and hours of its ordinary routine. Through seeking the divine will in its daily life, the prayerful soul also provides an "aperture" for the divine light to illumine and divinize the people and circumstances of its little corner of the world.

In the Judaeo-Christian tradition, this facet of spiritual growth, the interior absorbing of divine love and wisdom by being exposed to divinity radiating from the depths of an "other," was respected as a profound, though unexplainable, reality. This process was accepted as the usual method of God's self-revelation or manifestation, and the dynamic power of God's presence in more unusual circumstances was mitigated by a "go-between," who had been spiritually conditioned and was willing to act as an "ambassador" for his people.

" 'Speak to us yourself,' " they said to Moses, 'and we will listen; but do not let God speak to us or we shall die.' ... The people kept their distance while Moses approached the dark cloud where God was" (Exodus 20:19-21).

The Prophet, one in spirit with God, was receiver, carrier, and transmitter of God's Spirit and message. "The sons of Israel would see the face of Moses radiant" (Exodus 34:35). Just being in the presence of a soul transformed in divinity, veiled or buffered by humanity, was believed to be beneficial to spiritual growth, even though the experience was far beyond the ability of the created intellect to immediately comprehend. In time, through continued "being with," the disciple would be brought to clearer understanding like his master.

"Not by might and not by power, but by My spirit, says Yahweh" (Zechariah 4:1).

With the coming of Christ the master/disciple relationship reached perfection, for now Divine Nature Itself was embodied and made manifest. In the New Testament we find many vivid accounts of the soul's development through time spent in the presence of Christ, in which the simple loving gaze has absorbed God interiorly, even though the created intellect does not immediately understand what it "knows" (experiences/becomes).

"Peter spoke up, 'You are the Christ,' he said, 'the Son of the Living God.' Jesus replied, 'Simon son of Jonah, you are a happy man! Because it was not flesh and blood that revealed this to you [rational knowledge] but my Father in heaven' [infused mystical knowledge]" (Matthew 16:16).

"I bless You, Father, Lord of heaven and of earth, for hiding these things from the learned and the clever and revealing them to mere children" (Matthew 11:25).

The Apostles were first drawn to Jesus by the magnetic

power of Divinity, which touched their own inner divine spark. They did not follow Jesus because they agreed with His doctrine, for they did not immediately understand His teaching.

"They could make nothing of this: what He said was quite obscure to them, they had no idea what it meant" (Luke 18:34).

"But they did not understand what He said and were afraid to ask Him" (Mark 9:32).

Because of the faith and love of the Apostles they were receptive to the divine infusions. The teachings of Jesus were interiorized and stored, bypassing the created intellect. At the coming of the Spirit, like a bright light suddenly turned on in their interior storeroom, the Apostles were able to "see" all that they had been accumulating through the days, weeks, and months of the Master/disciple relationship.

"He then opened their minds to understand the Scriptures" (Luke 24:45).

Because the early Christians were familiar with the power of the Spirit and gradual enlightenment, "Scripture meditation" has always been held in the highest esteem. The Bible is not just a historical account but contains a spiritual treasury for the benefit of all people. The words of the Bible are divinely inspired and the prayerful soul will find ever-deeper meanings corresponding to its own growth in divine light. God's word is alive and active, able to touch the heart in different ways according to the individual.

"All Scripture is inspired by God and can profitably be used for teaching, for refuting error, for guiding people's lives and teaching them to be holy" (2 Timothy 3:16).

In Scripture meditation many people find it easy to relate interiorly to the divine presence, and move naturally into contemplative prayer without even being consciously aware of it, because they do not attempt to analyze their prayer, or try to label it, but have learned to "let go" with childlike simplicity.

The words of Jesus are addressed directly to each soul and they effect what they signify: "Fear not," "Your sins are forgiven," "Peace be with you," "As the Father has loved Me, so I have loved you." Inner discernment is the work of the spiritual faculties, and the Father's love is not just read about but, to the contemplative soul, "known" (experienced). At the awareness of this gracious reality, the soul is overwhelmed with gratitude, humbly conscious that as a mere creature it could never earn or deserve such love, but convinced that "God DOES love me anyway."

"God so loved the world" (John 3:16).

As love grows, the soul may relate in compassion with Jesus in the Garden, aware of His suffering for our sakes, His desolation and sense of abandonment: "Could you not watch one hour with Me?" (Matthew 26:40). This awareness touches a responsive chord, and the soul's love "goes out of itself," transcending time, to spiritually "be with" Him in His pain and loneliness. If death is called "the great equalizer," then certainly suffering and love are "common denominators" of the divine/human condition, through which we reach and touch and comfort each other.

Scripture meditation ("lectio divina" or divine reading) was often used for "discursive" meditation, as the prelude to "acquired" contemplation. At other times reading a Scripture passage, or often just a line that touches the heart, would be enough to immediately lift the prayerful soul into contemplation. Aware of its own inner need, the contemplative soul is able to identify with the needy who were drawn to Jesus during His earthly life.

"She had heard about Jesus, and she came up behind Him through the crowd and touched His cloak . . ." (Mark 5:27).

And Jesus said, "Who touched Me?"
It was I, Lord; I touched You.
I touched You with my weakness and with my many
    failures.

And in Your infinite kindness You turned to me
And You looked at me
And Your eyes wrapped me in Your mantle of Love!
For Your love is a greater good than life.

And Jesus said, "Who touched Me?"
It was I, Lord.
I touched You, for I have great need of You.
I have laid down my weapons, my pride and my anger
And stand defenseless and vulnerable,
Stand naked before You,
My every sore exposed
For I have nothing with which to clothe myself.
And You give me Your robe!
Your leper returns to give You thanks.
I give You my nothingness; You give me Your All.

And Jesus said, "Enter into My rest."
It is the movement of Love.
Love surges, love pulsates, love dilates, love enlarges,
Love inflames, love unifies, love transforms, even
though we are still.
For love is ever active
And the nature of love is to serve.

Because I was nothing You came to me.
You wrapped Your arms around my heart
To save me from myself.
Jesus, keep me always in the freedom of Your love
For I have fallen softly to sleep beneath Your shadow,
And my heart watches.

In other Scripture passages we share the joy of Mary Magdalene gazing lovingly at Jesus, aware of what she had been, but driven by divine love to what she could be, "because she has loved much she will be forgiven much." In God's "eyes" and "memory" love erases faults, for "love covers a multitude of sins."

"I it is, I it is, Who must blot out everything, and not remember your sins" (Isaiah 43:25).

God's love is always there but the soul must be able to receive it. The sun may be shining but if the shades are drawn the room will be in darkness. Many people, who have an enormous capacity for guilt, have found that placing their trust in the Lord and the prayerful reading of Scripture was the start of their personal "metanoia." It was also the beginning of inner healing, enabling them to accept and return the Father's love.

"So dear a son to Me, a child so favored, that after each threat of Mine I must still remember him, still be deeply moved for him, and let My tenderness yearn over him" (Jeremiah 31:20).

From the earliest days of contemplative communities, the relaxed state of the body conducive to contemplative prayer was found easier to attain after a number of hours spent in hard physical labor, which was a regular part of the daily schedule of monastery or convent life. Today, many people find that keeping still is much easier to accomplish after they have worked off their natural energies and, if they have sedentary jobs, may find walking, swimming, jogging, or yoga exercises helpful in relieving tensions before attempting to "rest in God."

As a helpful approach to contemplative prayer, many religions make use of the prayer of repetition: the Rosary, the mantra, the Tasbe (Moslem prayer beads similar to the Rosary), and others. By using the Rosary, the heart and soul meditate upon the Joyful, Sorrowful, and Glorious mysteries in the life of Christ, while the busy mind is kept occupied with reciting the prayers.

In the Christian tradition, in addition to the Rosary, there is the "Jesus Prayer," or the "Prayer of the Publican," which dates back to the early desert Fathers. "Lord Jesus Christ, Son of God, have mercy on me, a sinner." This prayer was repeated over and over again, synchronized with the breathing, to keep the soul aware of the presence of God while engaged in routine duties. In silent prayer, when all activity had ceased, the phrase would move from the lips and become a "prayer of the heart," like the Scripture passage in "acquired" contemplation. The Jesus prayer was also used to calm the busy mind, and gently lead it back after distractions.

In *The Wisdom of the Desert,* Thomas Merton wrote: "This illuminating term [quies or rest] has persisted in Greek monastic tradition as 'hesychia,' or 'sweet repose.' 'Quies' is a silent absorption aided by the soft repetition of a lone phrase of the Scriptures — the most popular being the prayer of the Publican. . . . In a shortened form this prayer became 'Lord have mercy' (Kyrie eleison) — repeated interiorly hundreds of times a day until it became as spontaneous and instinctive as breathing" (p. 20).

George Maloney, S.J., wrote in *The Breath of the Mystic,* "The Jesus prayer had its roots not only in the New Testament, but even farther back in the Old Testament. In the old covenant we see a developed personal conviction that the invocation of the Name of God brought about with it the conscious realization of His presence. 'Call on My name, I will hear' (Zechariah 13:9). Once a year on the Day of Atonement, Yahweh's name was pronounced only by the High Priest, who was chosen to offer sacrifice inside the Holy of Holies of the Temple of Jerusalem" (p. 87).

The Old Testament Jews would not pronounce the "Name" of Yahweh for they believed that to do so would call forth His presence. "Name," in ancient culture, was not simply a designation but a manifestation; therefore, the "Name" of God was actually considered to be the presence of God Himself. "Blessed is he who comes in the Name of the Lord," is one who radiates the Divine Presence or attributes, and the "Sign of the Cross" invokes the presence and blessing of the Trinity.

In the Christian tradition that sprang from this root, great care was taken to give an infant the name of a Saint at Baptism. The Baptismal name was believed to imbue the infant with the actual virtue and character of the person named.

Life-giving breath was synonymous with the Spirit of God, and was coordinated with the Jesus prayer, to consciously inhale divine life. "Inspire: to breathe, inhale; to motivate by divine influence."

"He misconceives the One Who shaped him, Who breathed an active soul into him and inspired a living spirit" (Wisdom 15:11).

In Greek, the word for "air" is "aura: an invisible emanation." In Latin "aura" means "breeze." The Hebrew word for "breath" and "spirit" is the same, "ruah," which is feminine. The soul is called the "sister" of God, of His very "essence."

"By His divine breath-like spiration, the Holy Spirit elevates the soul sublimely and informs her and makes her capable of breathing in God the same spiration of love that the Father breathes in the Son, and the Son in the Father, which is the Holy Spirit Himself, Who in the Father and the Son breathes out to her in this transformation, in order to unite her [soul] to Himself" (Spiritual Canticle, St. John of the Cross, St. 39:3).

The repetition of the Jesus prayer, while consciously breathing in divinity, was considered an earthly imitation of Trinitarian life. As an aid to participation in the spiration of the Trinity, the Jesus prayer can be simplified. It can be shortened to "Jesus, love," with the intention of breathing in "Jesus," and breathing out "Love"; or breathe in "Love" (Spirit), and breathe out "Jesus" (word).

The spiritual life of the contemplative soul is lived twenty-four hours a day. It is not something that is activated only on Sunday or during the time of prayer. It permeates one's whole existence as does the very breath we take. Prayer has been described as the breath of the soul, an activity without which the soul languishes.

Another approach to contemplative prayer, which has been gaining in popularity in recent years aided by the excellent writings on the subject, is "Centering Prayer," which makes use of one word to draw the attention inward to its center to rest in God.

"Simply sit, relaxed and quiet, enjoying your own inner calm and silence. . . . After a time, perhaps a single word will come: Jesus, Lord, Love, or any word that captures your response to His inner presence. Place into this word all your faith, your love, as you enter more and more deeply into Him. Slowly and effortlessly, repeat your word. Allow it to lead you more and more deeply into God's presence at the center of your being, where you are in God and God in you" (Finding Grace at the Center, Thomas Keating, OCSO; M. Basil Pennington, OCSO; Thomas E. Clarke, S.J., p. 63).

The members of religious orders were drawn to follow the spiritual path, or particular charism, of their founder or foundress. The various orders, in their beauty and diversity, reflect something of the beauty and immensity of God, just as individual souls do. St. Ignatius, the founder of the Jesuits, originated the "Spiritual Exercises," a step-by-step method of inner discernment and spiritual growth which has been found very helpful by both religious and laity, especially in "directed retreat" situations.

The fourteenth century work Cloud of Unknowing has inspired many souls to begin contemplative prayer. God is described as being behind a "cloud," and the soul is advised to put a "cloud of forgetting" between itself and the world and then direct its prayer, like darts of love, into the cloud where God dwells.

In addition to St. Teresa of Avila and St. John of the Cross, there are other Carmelites whose writings, or lives, have inspired many souls: St. Teresa Margaret, St. Therese of the Child Jesus, Bl. Lawrence of the Resurrection, Bl. Elizabeth of the Trinity, and Edith Stein, to name a few. Many souls have been led by the teachings or examples of St. Dominic, St. Thomas Aquinas, St. Catherine of Sienna, St. Benedict, St. Bernard, St. Francis of Assisi, St. Clare, St. Francis de Sales, St. Jane de Chantal, St. Bernadette, St. Margaret Mary; the list is endless. The charisms and graces bestowed by God upon the world, through individuals as His instruments, are for the benefit of all. The Saints, and all of the holy people in eternity that we admire, now loving with God's love, are eager to assist us as beloved younger sisters and brothers.

In the contemporary world, Thomas Merton, a Trappist, helped put "contemplation" back into America's vocabulary. In the late 1940's his best-selling book, *Seven Storey Mountain*, described Merton's own conversion experience. His readers took him to their hearts as he first discovered God, then overcame his doubts and accepted Him in faith, and finally abandoned his life to Him and entered the monastery. Merton described his progression from atheist to believer to contemplative, and many of his readers journeyed with him into contemplative prayer for the first time in their lives.

In the Carmelite tradition the approach to contemplative prayer recommended by St. Teresa of Avila was methodless and deceptively simple, prayer as relationship, a "friendship with Christ that grows into love." Friendship and love, being intrinsic to human nature, was considered by Teresa as possible for all, whether educated nobility or simple peasant.

"Since you are alone, strive to find a companion. Well what better Companion than the Master Himself. . . . Represent the Lord Himself as close to you and behold how lovingly and humbly He is teaching you. Believe me, you should remain with so good a Friend as long as you can. . . .

"He is not waiting for anything else, as He says to the bride, than that we look at Him. In the measure you desire Him, you will find Him" *(Way of Perfection,* St. Teresa of Avila, ch. 26:1, 3).

In her *Way of Perfection,* Teresa recommended meditating on the Lord's Prayer as a prelude to contemplative prayer. "It is very possible that while you are reciting the Our Father or some other vocal prayer, the

Lord may raise you to perfect contemplation. . . . The soul understands that without the noise of words this divine Master is teaching it by suspending its faculties, for if they were to be at work they would do harm rather than bring benefit. They are enjoying without understanding how they are enjoying. The soul is being enkindled in love, and it doesn't understand how it loves. It knows that it enjoys what it loves, but it doesn't know how. It clearly understands that this joy is not a joy the intellect obtains merely through desire. The will is enkindled without understanding how. . . . This good is a gift from the Lord of earth and heaven, who, in sum, gives according to who He is. What I have described, daughters, is perfect contemplation" (Ibid., ch. 25:1-2).

Teresa advises souls not to become impatient and seek the higher stages of prayer too soon, "For it is He who must bestow supernatural prayer, and He will grant it to you if you do not stop short on the road but try hard until you reach the end" (Ibid., ch. 25:4).

Drawing from her own experiences, and remembering her many difficulties, Teresa cautions: "It is very important for you to know that you are on the right road" (Ibid., ch. 22:3). "Because whether we like it or not, my daughters, we must all journey toward this fount, even though in different ways. Well, believe me, and don't let anyone deceive you by showing you a road other than that of prayer" (Ibid., ch. 21:6).

Through her own experience of divine union, Teresa realized the necessity of the surrender of human will to the divine will.

"Let us try hard to go against our own will in everything. For if you are careful, as I said, you will gradually without knowing how, find yourselves at the summit" (Ibid., ch. 12:3).

"Everything I have advised you about in this book is directed toward the complete gift of ourselves to the Creator, the surrender of our wills to His. . . . O my

Sisters, what strength lies in this gift! It does nothing less, when accompanied by the necessary determination, than draw the Almighty so that He becomes one with our lowliness, transforms us into Himself, and effects a union of the Creator with the creature" [Ibid., ch. 32:9, 11].

For Teresa, Jesus was a real person, a dear friend, and not just an abstract idea. This person-to-person relationship, with its devotion to the humanity of Christ and ensuing love, was the foundation and guiding light of her soul's journey. But, for a time in her prayer life, Teresa began to have doubts. The popular books of the day, that gave advice on how to pray, recommended that the mind be freed of all images. Teresa described the problems she encountered when trying to follow their advice.

"They say that in the case of those who are advancing, these corporeal images, even when referring to the humanity of Christ, are an obstacle or impediment to the most perfect contemplation. . . . In my opinion this practice is why many souls, when they reach the prayer of union, do not advance further or attain a very great freedom of spirit" [Life, St. Teresa of Avila, ch. 22:1, 5].

Teresa wrote that the Lord guided her back to the right path by "sending me someone who would draw me away from this error," and she returned to her former way of prayer. "Since the soul receives permission to remain at the feet of Christ, it should endeavor not to leave that place . . . let it imitate the Magdalene" [Ibid., ch. 22:12].

"What a pity it was for me to have left You, my Lord, under the pretext of serving You more! . . . Oh, what a bad road I was following, Lord! Now it seems to me I was walking on no path until You brought me back, for in seeing You at my side I saw all blessings. . . . Whoever lives in the presence of so good a friend and excellent a leader, who went ahead of us to be the first to suffer, can endure all things. The Lord helps us, strengthens us, and never fails: He is a true friend. . . . God desires that if we are going to please Him and receive His great favors, we must do so

115

through the most sacred humanity of Christ, in Whom He takes His delight . . . we must enter by this gate . . . desire no other path even if you are at the summit of contemplation; on this road you walk safely" (Ibid., ch. 22:6-7).

"I started again to love the most sacred humanity. Prayer began to take shape as an edifice that now had a foundation" (Ibid., ch. 24:2).

In contemplative prayer through the ages the disciple/soul still follows its Master/Jesus.

7

The Effects
of Contemplative Prayer

Unfortunately, religion and spirituality have often had a "bad press." Little boys who go to church or Sunday School are frequently portrayed as "sissies." The "real he-men" never go to church (especially in Westerns) except under protest, and then it is always a source of humor. In Westerns it is the "little woman" who usually insists on attending church, but it is understood that the "hero" is only humoring her, and will slip out at the first opportunity.

What is too often depicted as a "religious" person in books, movies, television, etc., is a distorted stereotype, one of the childhood false images carried over into an adult environment. In most cases the portrayal is the exact opposite of what an authentically spiritual person would be. The supposedly religious character is often puritanical, devoid of humor, rigid, legalistic, and completely unappealing — certainly not one to inspire imitation.

In truth, authentic spirituality has exactly the opposite effect, expanding and opening the inner self to a limitless universe. The "freedom of the children of God" is more than a pious statement. There are no boundaries for the soul that is one with God, Who is infinite freedom. Earthly life and love, and the beauty of creation are enjoyed in the purest, therefore most intense forms, unclouded by human distortion. "God saw all He had made, and indeed it was very good" (Genesis 1:31).

Natural, human vision has been compared to walking down a road, and passing houses, trees, and other objects one at a time. The "eternal now" of God could be pictured as having a panoramic view from a plane, seeing the past, present, and future simultaneously. The contemplative soul, in its oneness with God, sees the world with God's eyes, and in that divine contemplative gaze loves the world as God loves it, and desires for the world what God desires, a restored, harmonious, transformed world united with Himself.

"When that day comes — it is Yahweh Who speaks — she will call me, 'My husband' " (Hosea 2:18).

The contemplative soul, with its God-vision, is spiritually "present" at the beginning of creation, when the earth was new. Every end is a beginning. The soul came from Paradise and is meant to return to Paradise. The contemplative soul briefly glimpses the return to Eden here and now, for it is a citizen of both earth and heaven.

The ever-deepening union of the contemplative soul places it, as it were, upon the vantage point of divinity, with its wisdom and insight. From this height it sees not only the travelled road and its present condition, but a hint of what is in store, what God has planned since the beginning of time — "what eye has not seen and ear has not heard," but what has been tasted at the edge of perception. These brief sublime experiences incite contemplative souls into "straining forward to what is beyond," to the eternal possession of the ALL.

Paradoxically, the contemplative soul at the same time loves and appreciates the created world and the sacred value of the present moment. In the heart of the contemplative there exists, simultaneously, a commitment to effort on the part of the Kingdom, and the conviction that everything is in the hands of God; a sense of urgency, and a deep, peaceful acceptance; an awareness of the world's present needs, and the unshakeable belief that all will be accomplished in God's time and according to His plan.

Since the beginning of time mankind has dreamed of becoming god-like but, in its pride, has usually tried to accomplish this goal in its own time and its own way. The "Tower of Babel" represents man attempting to achieve heaven completely through his own efforts. The Egyptian pharaohs prepared for eternal life through elaborate tombs and preservation techniques. Today there are many people who plan on having their bodies frozen, with the hope that they will be revived in the future. Eternal life is guaranteed, but often seems little understood. Through God's generous self-giving love He desires to share His divine, eternal life with His children. When we spiritually "come of age," we will receive our inheritance. "There is no need to be afraid, little flock, for it has pleased your Father to give you the Kingdom" (Luke 12:32).

Earthly life is meant to prepare us for "entering" or participating, in this Kingdom. Without growth in divine love, the soul obviously would not be "like" God and, therefore, would be incapable of participation. Regular contemplative prayer could be compared to lining up our inner selves daily with a spiritual "test pattern," Jesus. Human nature in daily life tends to get "off course" or distorted, but through continually "zeroing in" on the beams of Love, the wandering soul is eventually drawn home to its Source. It is a lifetime journey and in spite of interruptions and setbacks, and sometimes mainly because of them, the soul's determination grows.

In every culture throughout history, myths, legends, fables, and fairy stories have expressed the deepest longings of humanity to transcend its natural state. The Divine signals from within have been sensed, but often not clearly understood. The creative Spirit has inspired the human race to represent the spiritual, little-known, mystical dimension of its existence symbolically in song and story.

Some of the basic examples are: the need to overcome a "dragon" or "beast"· through love and acceptance to transform the beast (or frog) into a long-lost prince or princess; to win a kingdom and/or marriage with a princess by successfully completing a hazardous journey into an unknown land; or by a search for a royal person, who had been lost or kidnapped, and forced to live as a lowly servant.

The "ugly duckling" transformed into a beautiful swan, or the "Cinderella" experience, rather vividly symbolizes the spiritual progression of the soul, from its exile to its exaltation. The soul is portrayed as lost and unhappy, unable to participate in a loving existence. Through the "magic" of love, the drab, tattered outward appearance is transformed to reveal the true nature of the inner person. Through the generous, outpouring nature of love, the riches of the King are bestowed upon the lowly soul, clothing it in the King's own splendor and making it as dazzling as the King Himself, thereby enabling the soul to participate in and enjoy the Kingdom, and to "live happily ever after."

In the Bible the Parable of the Prodigal Son is another approach. Jesus tells His listeners that the inheritance is lost through the self-centeredness of the son, and his renouncing of the Father's will in favor of his own. After experiencing his own emptiness, by being "brought low," the son gains perception. Through his growth in wisdom he realizes that his Father's will was not confining but enriching. The parable portrays the need for "metanoia," a change of heart or new way of seeing, as a requirement for participating in the Kingdom. Without this conversion experience, the soul is like a "Sleeping Beauty," that needs the kiss of love to awaken its divine faculties.

Our destiny of being "like" God will only be accomplished in God's time and in God's own way. But the spiritual life is not only a promise of future reward, it is an awakening and enjoyment here and now of the latent potential hidden deep in the mystery of humanity.

"I will give you the hidden treasures, the secret hoards" (Isaiah 45:3).

"I, Yahweh, your God, teach you what is good for you, I lead you in the way that you must go. If only you had been alert to my commandments, your happiness would have been like a river, your integrity like the waves of the sea" (Isaiah 48:18).

The initial efforts of preparation are up to each individual, and the attitude of willingness to proceed in faith and trust, respecting God's way, just as we abide by the laws of nature when we tend our gardens.

We clear the "earth" of weeds and rocks, soften the hard outer crust, and allow the tender shoots of the new, divine self to break through into light, dawn, spring, Resurrection. We do not dig up the seeds every few days to see if there is progress, but respectfully wait without interfering, while God's sun and rain do their work. While no one would think of taking credit for the tree or the beautiful blossoms, we also realize that if we had not prepared the earth the seed would have had little chance.

No one can explain to us how a gigantic tree or a beautiful flower can be contained in a tiny seed, but we are used to the idea and accept it. An electrical engineer can explain "how" electricity works, but not "why." Astronomers are able to chart and study only the nearest stars and planets, and speculate on distant stars and other galaxies. From this they admit to an unending universe that they may never be able to measure or explain, yet they believe in its existence.

The same principle holds true in the spiritual world as it does in the natural world. We may never know or understand all of the answers during our earthly life. What we know of God and divine life is what He chose to reveal to us in order to ensure our spiritual development. We are to accept the rest in faith, until we are filled with the wisdom of God.

Most children, at one time or other, would try to picture eternity, saying "forever, and ever, and ever," finally giving up with no hope of understanding infinity. It is more than the created mind can grasp, for here on earth we are bound by the laws of time, space, and gravity, and cannot envision an "eternal now," or beings of pure spirit with no limitations.

It is difficult for human, created minds to grasp the idea of existence in a different dimension, or another state of being. Human language and reasoning fall short in this attempt. Vague fears of the unknown spiritual area of humanity cause uneasiness and confusion, and many people dread the thought of death as "the end," when in reality it is another beginning, a birth of spirit. Again, it is necessary to use our inner vision, and see beyond surface appearances.

The regular practice of contemplative prayer cannot be emphasized enough as the means of activating our inner vision and developing a heart-to-heart relationship with the Indwelling God, Who then draws us through love to Transforming Union. Everyone receives an equal "share" of divinity at conception, but the degree of awareness of this divine life within varies during our earthly journey. As we begin to recognize the divine within ourselves, divinity becomes "familiar" to the soul, and we recognize God in every other human being, and in all creation.

"Anybody who is convinced that he belongs to Christ must go on to reflect that we all belong to Christ no less than he does" (2 Corinthians 10:7).

Human nature is fragile and wounded and, if left to itself, would find little meaning in life. Spiritual growth leads it from the dark prison of self into the light of God's love, where it grows and blossoms into what it was created to be — like God. Souls are like flowers, meant to instinctively turn toward the Sun of love. Without that life-giving light there is no growth. "Self is the only prison that can ever bind the soul" (VanDyke).

"Out of His infinite glory, may He give you the power through His Spirit for your hidden self to grow strong, so that Christ may live in your hearts through faith, and then, planted in love and built on love, you will with all the saints have strength to grasp the breadth and the length, the height and the depth; until, knowing the love of Christ, which is beyond all knowledge, YOU ARE FILLED WITH THE UTTER FULLNESS OF GOD. Glory be to Him Whose power, working in us, can do infinitely more than we can ask or imagine" (Ephesians 3:16).

Studies have shown that we only retain a small percentage of what we read or hear. It is not enough to read or hear about the spiritual life; we also have to live it in order to effect an interior change. A French philosopher stated, "If you do not live the way that you believe, you will soon begin to believe the way that you live."

We are body, mind, and spirit. These three areas cannot be isolated or compartmentalized, and they necessarily affect each other. To ignore the development of any one area of our humanity is detrimental to the other two. It is ironic that the most important area, the eternal spirit, is the one most often neglected. The mind is thoroughly educated, the body developed through the growing interest in nutrition and exercise, while too often the spirit languishes.

"Physical exercises are useful enough, but the usefulness of spirituality is unlimited, since IT HOLDS OUT THE REWARD OF LIFE HERE AND NOW AND OF THE FUTURE AS WELL" (1 Timothy 4:8).

Authentic spiritual development leads to wholeness; it is psychologically sound. For wholeness, the three areas of humanity, body, mind, and spirit, must be healthy, balanced, and integrated. It is most beneficial if they are developing simultaneously throughout earthly life.

The force of God's love is immeasurable and our divine spark contains the seed of this power, meant to propel us to Him. Spirit will only be content with Spirit, "deep calls unto deep." Being of God's "essence," this deepest part of ourselves cannot be satisfied with anything less than God. To attempt to alleviate the hunger and thirst of the spirit with earthly satisfactions would be like diverting a rocket from its course.

The divine spark within us longs to return to its Source, our Father. We are homesick for heaven and oneness, and will always feel the pull of the "Divine Magnet," which gives rise to inexplicable stirrings of love and restless longing. Paradoxically, this is a help in our prayer life, a homing instinct, which draws us back to our Source. We become like that which we hunger for, like that which we love, as we slowly but surely wend our way home.

"Our homeland is in heaven" (Philippians 3:21).

"Our hearts were made for Thee, O Lord, and they will be restless until they rest in Thee" (St. Augustine).

Inner restlessness is part of the human condition. Many people are confused by these inner longings and try to escape through constant noise and activity. In today's world, suicide has even become a frequent means of escape. People often do not realize that their anguish is in the spirit, not the body, and that the death of the body will not eliminate their suffering, because the soul, like God, is infinite.

The soul comes forth from God and returns to God, at a time that only He knows. During earthly life, through exercise of free will, the soul actively participates in its ongoing growth and development. Our humanity provides the environment, time, and opportunity to receive the infusion of divinity, contingent upon our agreement, at a rate equivalent to our capacity. Our human nature, like a protective covering, safeguards the soul from a too-sudden merging with Divinity before it is fully prepared, as would happen if life were abruptly ended through one's own decision.

"Purgatory" is the term used to describe the state of a soul in need of further purifying and strengthening before uniting with God. There is a long-held belief that such a soul must endure further purification passively, for after death there are no more free choices, for good or evil. But just how this process is completed in the soul that prematurely enters eternity is a mystery. The Saints, through their transformation experiences, were only able to describe the successfully completed journey.

Some people hope that another person will alleviate their spiritual longing and may enter marriage expecting more from their partner than what is humanly possible, blaming their partner when the inner restlessness returns. But the deepest part of our selves is reserved for God alone; it is "part" of Him and can only "rest" in Him. "Even at home, I am homesick" (Chesterton).

Just being aware of the nature of our inner conflicts and that we are no different from any other human being is in itself comforting, for it lessens the fear of the unknown. Our personal love relationship with God will not immunize nor protect us from pain and suffering, but it will help us to grow in understanding and thereby see things in their proper perspective. If we understood spiritual development as well as we understand physical development, we would not be so fearful or confused by the workings of God in the soul.

By "putting on the mind of Christ," we are able to see the whole picture instead of merely fragments. Through the divine outlook we begin to see with a "wide-angle lens" instead of having "microscopic vision." God pries the colored pebbles from our tightly clenched fists, and fills our empty, waiting hands with priceless jewels. God shapes us and empties us only in order to fill us with Himself. As fire transforms into itself everything that it touches, our souls gradually become one with Divine Fire.

"This purgative and loving knowledge or divine light we are speaking of, has the same effect on a soul that fire has on a log of wood. The soul is purged and prepared for transformation into the fire. Fire, when applied to wood, first dehumidifies it, dispelling all moisture and making it give off any water it contains. . . . By drying out the wood, the fire brings to light and expels all those ugly and dark accidents which are contrary to fire. Finally, by heating and enkindling it from without the fire transforms the wood into itself and makes it as beautiful as it is itself. Once transformed, the wood no longer has any activity or passivity of its own, except for its weight and its quantity which is denser than the fire. FOR IT POSSESSES THE PROPERTIES AND PERFORMS THE ACTIONS OF FIRE" (*Dark Night,* St. John of the Cross, Bk. II, ch. 10:1).

We are not given full access to the divine light within us until our wills are completely aligned with divine will. We have all heard of people who may have started their spiritual journey with good intentions, but through pride and a desire for power, began directing the love of their followers to themselves instead of to God. The purification process refines the will, restoring it to divine compatibility. The enlightened soul that has surrendered itself fully to God will be entrusted with spiritual treasures, as the child that has matured and gained adult wisdom will be trusted to wisely manage his or her inheritance.

As we grow in the realization of being loved and accepted by God, it brings inner healing and ever-increasing freedom. Free from concern about our image, the false self gradually disappears as we surrender our self-will and self-centeredness and completely abandon ourselves to God's will, becoming centered in Him. We are aware of our human weaknesses and failings, our limitations, but we can love and accept ourselves through God's having first loved us.

As we love and accept ourselves, we are then able to love and accept others, and as we grow in compassion for others there is a new gentleness with ourselves. Sincerely trying to improve, we do not become overly upset if we fail now and then, for we know that in spite of our mistakes, God looks at our hearts and sees our intentions. All that He asks of us is that we are faithful and keep trying; the rest is up to God. We can let go of the idea of "perfecting" ourselves, for our spiritual progress is God's doing, not ours, and there is a sense of relief in that acceptance.

The prayerful soul is alive to the many ways that God is

present which previously might have slipped by unnoticed. God often "surfaces" interiorly, Living Water welling up from our depths. "Behold, I stand at the door and knock." In contemplative prayer we open the door and descend into the secret room in our deepest center, the inner sanctum where God dwells.

"When you pray, go to your private room and, when you have shut your door, pray to your Father Who is in that secret place" (Matthew 6:6).

Prayer is the entry into the vast reaches of inner space where we learn to let go and gradually descend, to experience the deep calm, the incredible stillness, and cosmic silence beyond time which is a dimension of our inter-connectedness with Divinity and each other — the non-verbal communing of saints. Human spirit immerses itself in Living Water emerging cleansed and refreshed and there is a progressive healing of the inner wounds. Each time we surface to be present to time-oriented activity we are different, retaining something of our inner harmony which accumulates in non-measurable fashion. "Man's mind stretched by a new idea never goes back to its original dimensions" (Oliver Wendell Holmes). Man's soul, plunged however briefly into the depths of Divine Love, is never exactly the same.

"We must try to penetrate our most secret self, and examine our being from all sides. Let us try, patiently, to perceive the ocean of forces to which we are subjected and in which our growth is, as it were, steeped . . . for the depth and universality of our dependence on so much altogether outside our control all go to make up the embracing intimacy of our communion with the world to which we belong" (The Divine Milieu, Teilhard de Chardin, p. 76).

"And so, for the first time in my life perhaps (although I am supposed to meditate every day!), I took the lamp and, leaving the zone of everyday occupations and relationships where everything seems clear, I went down into my inmost self, to the deep abyss whence I feel dimly that my

127

power of action emanates. But as I moved further and further away from the conventional certainties by which social life is superficially illuminated, I became aware that I was losing contact with myself" *(Ibid.,* p. 77).

"At each step of the descent a new person was disclosed within me of whose name I was no longer sure, and who no longer obeyed me. And when I had to stop my exploration because the path faded from beneath my steps, I found a bottomless abyss at my feet, and out of it came — arising I know not from where — the current which I dare to call 'my' life. . . . My self is given to me far more than it is formed by me. . . . Stirred by my discovery, I then wanted to return to the light of day and forget the disturbing enigma in the comfortable surroundings of familiar things — to begin living again at the surface.

"And if something saved me, it was hearing the voice of the Gospel, guaranteed by divine successes, speaking to me from the depth of the night: 'It is I, be not afraid.' Yes, O God, I believe it: and I believe it all the more willingly because it is not only a question of my being consoled, but of my being completed: it is You Who are the origin of the impulse, and at the end of that continuing pull which all my life long I can do no other than follow" *(Ibid.,* p. 78).

"In the life which wells up in me and in the matter which sustains me, I find much more than your gifts. It is You Yourself Whom I find, You Who makes me participate in Your being, You Who molds me. . . . O God, Whose call precedes the very first of our movements, grant me the desire to desire being — that, by means of that divine thirst which is your gift, the access to the great waters may open wide within me" *(Ibid.,* p. 79).

"If any man is thirsty, let him come to Me!" (John 7:37).

St. Augustine said, "Give me a man who loves and he will understand." In union with God we are one with every person, with nature, and with the universe. The loving gaze of the soul "sees" (experiences) God at the heart of all creation. Through oneness with God St. Francis of

Assisi was inspired to write his beautiful *Canticle to the Sun*, and the mystical poet, St. John of the Cross, was intensely moved by the traces and reflections of the divine presence, what Chardin called "the diaphany of the Divine at the heart of the universe on fire."

"My Beloved is the mountains, and lonely wooded valleys, Strange islands, and resounding rivers, The whistling of love-stirring breezes, The tranquil night at the time of the rising dawn, Silent music, Sounding solitude, The supper that refreshes, and deepens love" *(Spiritual Canticle*, St. John of the Cross, 14, 15). "Mine are the heavens and mine is the earth. Mine are the nations, the just are mine, and mine the sinners. The angels are mine, and the Mother of God, and all things are mine: and God Himself is mine and for me, because Christ is mine and all for me" *(Prayer of a Soul Taken With Love*, St. John of the Cross).

The poet Gerard Manley Hopkins, S.J., wrote, "The world is charged with the grandeur of God," and Elizabeth Barrett Browning described it, "Every common bush afire with God, and he who sees removes his shoes, the rest sit around and pluck blackberries." "Happy the eyes that see what you see" (Luke 10:23).

Not only is our final transformation in God to be revered but all of the means to that end, which are also divine gifts or sacraments since they came from the hands of God. To respond to the visible beauty of the created world enables the soul to soar more readily to that which is hinted at but invisible.

"O world invisible, we view thee, O world intangible, we touch thee, O world unknowable, we know thee, Inapprehensible, we clutch thee! . . . The angels keep their ancient places; Turn but a stone, and start a wing! Tis ye, tis your estranged faces, That miss the many-splendoured thing" (Francis Thompson).

The Holy Spirit is creative and enlightening. With growth in Spirit and the new way of seeing, the soul's creativity increases. There is a remarkable similarity between the creative vision and process, and contemplation. The artist, by using ordinary materials and everyday subjects and applying inner vision, provides a fresh interpretation of the familiar, an alternate way of seeing. Through an inner relating and self-expression, the artist enables the interested observer to see "reality" in a new way, through the eyes of the artist. A person or setting that may have previously gone unnoticed is seen thereafter in a different light. In a sense, it is similar to the way the Saints have highlighted certain aspects of the Gospel, and by lifting them out of the context of the familiar put them in a new perspective.

For twenty years I have been a lay member of the Discalced Carmelites, a contemplative Order. From the beginning, I sensed that being an artist had predisposed me for contemplative prayer, but I did not know why. I did know that the same state of consciousness was experienced whether in meditation or painting a picture.

Artists in describing their artistic process sound as if they are talking about meditation. They speak of entering another level of consciousness, involving a new way of seeing, and of being "at one" with the subject. While creating, a sense of timelessness is experienced, with the feeling of being relaxed but alert and very aware. There is a sense of being detached from any noise or activity going on around them; they may be aware of people talking but it doesn't register, and they do not feel compelled to respond.

To an artist all faces are beautiful, for the artist instinctively goes beyond surface appearances to the real "being" within. The artist, by "gazing at" the subject, absorbs and becomes one with the subject, feeling and identifying with each human condition, making it a part of the artist's inner self. This interior relating then becomes outward expression in a painting, music, sculpture, writing, acting, dancing, etc. A group of painters portraying the same model will reveal individual interpretations, similar to the way that we each reflect our unique Divine Image, combined with self.

The artist is receptive, open and unbiased, reverently accepting what is presented to its inner gaze, appreciating the splendor of a blossoming tree, or a timeworn face without being judgmental or controlling. This inner gaze seeks the core of reality of each person, tree, animal, or rock, in order to express the uniqueness of that particular one.

Creativity is not confined to the obvious areas of artistic endeavor, but applies to every person and every activity. A new way of seeing is needed for those seeking cures for the sick, or for feeding the hungry, or building new cities, as well as the teacher showing students that learning can be fun, the cook preparing an enjoyable meal, the gardener tending the plants, or enjoying a peaceful walk after a spring rain. Clarity of vision influences attitude, developing a gentle courteousness, a sense of the inner link with every other human being, with animals, and the earth.

Creative thinking is the opposite of destructive thinking, a positive building up and restoring, as opposed to a negative tearing down or condemning. The creative approach is, in itself, enjoyable, making work interesting and fulfilling rather than boring or dehumanizing.

Now there may be not only a scientific explanation for the relationship between creativity and contemplation, but also the assurance that the creative predisposition for prayer is possible for everyone. Betty Edwards, a California art teacher, in her doctoral thesis reports her observations based on studies carried out during the 50's and 60's at the California Institute of Technology. A team of scientists headed by Dr. Roger W. Sperry (one of three Americans awarded the 1981 Nobel Prize in medicine, and a member of the Pontifical Academy of Science) conducted experiments on the left and right hemispheres of the brain. Results of these experiments, to reduce the violent seizures of a group of epileptic patients, revealed that the left and right hemispheres of the brain receive and process information differently.

The "major" left hemisphere is analytical, verbal, logical, factual, sequential, and time-oriented. These are all traits that are generally categorized as "masculine."

The "minor" right hemisphere is intuitive, holistic, understands metaphors and seemingly unrelated ideas, is time-free, and able to live with mystery. It would seem that the intuitive "feminine" side is able to accept what it does not thoroughly understand, and is able to absorb and assimilate into its being the unexplainable mystery of God. Since these "right-hemisphere" traits are basic to the nature of woman, perhaps they could help to explain the predominance of women at most religious functions. The analytical, logical "masculine" left hemisphere, basic to the nature of man, often requires reasons and facts before it proceeds step by step.

The masculine and feminine sides of the brain are able to operate individually, and also harmoniously together, as men and women are able to do. The worldly man who, consciously or subconsciously, believes himself superior to women, represses all of the traits which are considered "feminine," seeing in them a sign of "weakness," and consequently inhibits spiritual development in the feminine side of his soul. This does not seem to be a problem for men who are spiritual and/or creative. The humble man, who looks down on no one, is open to all of the growth-inducing reflections radiating from the depths of others. The worldly man, believing the feminine inferior, blocks them out. We cannot accept half of God's reflection, and reject the other half. The Image would be lopsided.

"Let US make mankind in OUR OWN IMAGE, in the likeness of Ourselves . . . male and female He created them" (Genesis 1:26-27).

The masculine and feminine aspects of divinity and humanity cannot be ignored. In creating human beings male and female, God established separate functions within His physical laws of nature. Man and woman, equal but different, each reflect a unique aspect of Divinity through their particular state of being. In addition, there is present in the very essence of the soul a spiritual "twin" or completely "other," as a potential to be developed. Since the soul is of the essence of God, this latent potential contains divine attributes or traits which must be fully developed and integrated in order to reflect the harmonious completeness of the Trinity. The majesty, power, and might of God need to be balanced with His gentleness, forgiveness, compassion, humility, and all of the traits that are not much admired nor sought after by the worldly.

Male and female are not meant to compete but to complement and perfect each other. There must be reverence and respect, and a willingness to assist one another in growing in the love of God, which in turn deepens mutual love. We live our "yes" to the ancient question, "Am I my brother's [sister's] keeper?" The love of husband and wife, accepting each other as equals, encourages the growth of the spiritual opposite. The spiritual growth of the individual soul, reflecting to the best of its ability the many facets of God, is brought by divine love to the supernatural state of being His "equal" and bride.

"For the property of love is to make the lover equal to the object loved. Since the soul in this state possesses perfect love, she is called the BRIDE OF THE SON OF GOD, WHICH SIGNIFIES EQUALITY WITH HIM. In this equality of friendship the possessions of both are held in common, as the Bridegroom Himself said to His disciples: 'I have now called you My friends, because all that I have heard from My Father I have manifested to you'" (Spiritual Canticle, St. John of the Cross, St. 28:1).

Spirit operates through, but is not confined or restricted by, the mind and body. Just as grace builds on nature, spirit builds on our innate human tendencies or qualities. The function and traits of the left and right hemispheres of the brain seem to parallel another invisible reality, the dual spiritual nature of the soul. To become God's counterpart, both sides of the soul must be brought to completion. For wholeness and fullness of life, both sides of the brain and all of their positive traits should be developed.

"The creative process has feminine quality, and the creative work arises from unconscious depths" *(Modern Man in Search of a Soul,* C.G. Jung, p. 170).

The world of science affirms the masculine/feminine aspects of the physical brain, just as it has previously affirmed, through psychology, the invisible masculine/feminine potential of the spirit. Carl Jung described the latent masculine "animus" in women, and the latent feminine "anima" in men, as "the other side of the soul's life." Following the psychological path, Jung arrived at the same conclusions as did many Saints and spiritual writers through their spiritual journey.

"The self, therefore, is the God within." "Only the man who can consciously assent to the power of the inner voice becomes a personality" *(Collected Works,* C.G. Jung).

"Among all my patients in the second half of life — that is to say, over thirty-five — there has not been one whose problem in the last resort was not that of finding a religious outlook on life. It is safe to say that every one of them fell ill because he had lost that which the living religions of every age have given to their followers, and none of them has been really healed who did not regain his religious outlook. A spiritual need has produced in our time our 'discovery' of psychology" *(Modern Man in Search of a Soul,* C.G. Jung, pp. 201, 229).

"The inner voice is the voice of a fuller life, of a wider, more comprehensive consciousness" *(The Development of Personality,* C.G. Jung).

The contemplative soul lives on the edge of the future, for its life is in God Who exists beyond the limitations of time. The contemplative soul lives in a state of readiness, perceiving a distant thunder, a sense of imminence, a prelude of that which is to come, misted by time and not clearly defined, but prepared for and calmly awaited.

8

Tracing the Spiritual Journey

Spiritual development, like life, is a whole, and its various components cannot actually be isolated or limited. It is basically a journey in love, and love is not subject to analysis. The activity of love is cohesive, to draw together and unite. The ever-growing divine love in the human spirit (agape) and the ever-increasing clarity of its divine reflection inevitably pull the divine and human together, and the perfected soul merges with God in sameness.

The two Carmelite Mystical Doctors, St. Teresa of Jesus (more popularly known as St. Teresa of Avila) and St. John of the Cross, were inspired by God to describe the soul's spiritual development — insofar as spiritual matters can be described. In their writings Teresa and John made use of various analogies in an attempt to explain the emptying and filling process of the spiritual journey, and the state of the soul undergoing that process, in order to reassure the many souls who would be having similar experiences. Teresa and John both believed that it was essential for souls to know that they were on the right road, for spiritual suffering was intensified by their concern that they might be going astray, and by fear of the unknown.

"If the Lord leads it [soul] along the path of fear, as He did me, it is a great trial if there is no one to understand it. To see itself described brings it intense joy, and then it sees clearly the path it is walking on. It is a great good to know what one must do in order to advance in any of these stages. For I have suffered much and have lost a great deal of time for not knowing what to do, and I pity souls greatly who find themselves alone when they arrive at this stage" (*Life*, St. Teresa of Avila, ch. 14:7).

St. John of the Cross wrote: "If there is no one to understand these persons, they either turn back and abandon the road or lose courage. . . . They fatigue and overwork themselves, thinking that they are failing because of their negligences or sins. [Discursive] Meditation is now useless for them, because God is conducting them along another road, which is contemplation and which is very different from the first. . . . Those who are in this situation should feel comforted; they ought to persevere patiently and not be afflicted. Let them trust in God Who does not fail those who seek Him with a simple and righteous heart; nor does He fail to impart what is needful for the way until getting them to the clear and pure light of love" (*The Dark Night*, St. John of the Cross, Bk. I, ch. 10:2-3).

In *The Interior Castle*, Teresa represents the journey to union with God as a gradual progression from the outer rooms of the castle — the soul — to its deepest center, the inner room where God dwells. In his *Spiritual Canticle*, St. John of the Cross presents basically the same journey, but his description was inspired by the Canticle of Canticles in the Old Testament. The bride/soul longs for the Bridegroom/God and her ever-increasing desire, like a purifying fire, prepares her for ever-increasing love.

Both writings describe the beginning soul's awareness of an inner darkness; the painful purifying of the desert or dark night in which the soul is emptied of imperfections in order to be filled with Divine love and light; and the delightful joy of the "touches" or "wounds of love" during those times that the infusions take place. These are sometimes accompanied by raptures, ecstasies, or levitations, as the force of divine love sweeps the soul off its feet, so to speak. The enjoyment of the touches of love may be brief and passing, but the effects are permanent. With each touch the soul is more deeply immersed in God. When the soul has reached the highest state attainable in this life the sufferings and fears of the purifying stages are over, and the raptures and ecstasies cease, for the perfected soul now operates with divine love and strength.

"Love will come to its perfection in us when we can face the day of Judgment without fear; because EVEN IN THIS WORLD WE HAVE BECOME AS HE IS. In love there can be no fear, but fear is driven out by perfect love: because to fear is to expect punishment, and anyone who is afraid is still imperfect in love" (1 John 4:17). "It is impossible to combine the love of a son with the fear of a slave" (1 John 4:17g).

The unusual experiences of St. Teresa of Avila helped to more clearly define the various phases of the soul's spiritual journey. A definite pattern emerged and was recorded. For the first time the different levels of spiritual development and the condition of the soul within those states were described from the soul's firsthand experience.

Because the two most complete descriptions of the soul's journey to union with God were written by Carmelites, this spiritual path is often called the "Carmelite way." Actually, it is more universal. The Scriptures disclose that the Apostles also attained the state of spiritual marriage. If the Apostles had described their spiritual journeys we would have had earlier records which would, no doubt, have been similar to Teresa and John. God leads each soul uniquely and it perceives the journey in its own fashion, but the basic progression through stages of purification and enlightenment, the sunshine and shadow on the spiritual path, is the same.

The "metanoia" or conversion of Paul was preceded by a "Transfiguration experience."

"The members of the Sanhedrin all looked intently at Stephen, and his face appeared to them like the face of an angel. . . . Stephen, filled with the Holy Spirit, gazed into heaven and saw the glory of God, and Jesus standing at God's right hand. . . . As they were stoning him, Stephen said in invocation, 'Lord Jesus, receive my spirit.' . . . Saul entirely approved of the killing" (Acts 6:15, 7:55, 59).

Paul does not directly refer to this event when describing his metanoia, but a grace-filled experience such as this must have touched him in his depths. God works in the soul whether or not the intellect is consciously aware of His activity. God is always waiting for the least sign of compassion or love, an opening to the soul; and the Spirit, like water, not only seeps in but enlarges the opening. Through this crack in the soul's defenses the divine rays begin to awaken the latent potential of the soul.

"Meanwhile Saul was still breathing threats to slaughter the Lord's disciples. . . . Suddenly, while he was travelling to Damascus and just before he reached the city, there came a light from heaven all around him. He fell to the ground, and then he heard a voice saying, 'Saul, Saul, why are you persecuting me?' 'Who are you, Lord?' he asked, and the voice answered, 'I am Jesus, and you are persecuting me. Get up now and go into the city, and you will be told what you have to do.' The men travelling with Saul stood there speechless, for though they heard the voice they could see no one. Saul got up from the ground, but even with his eyes wide open he could see nothing at all, and they had to lead him into Damascus by the hand. For three days he was without his sight, and took neither food nor drink" (Acts 9:1, 3).

This encounter of the spiritually unprepared soul with the powerful presence of Divinity had a traumatic, although temporary, physical effect upon Paul and placed him instantaneously in the dark night of the senses. It was such a sudden change of direction that the other disciples were still afraid of him; "they could not believe he was really a disciple" (Acts 9:27). But Barnabas "explained how the Lord had appeared to Saul and spoken to him on his journey, and how he had preached boldly at Damascus in the name of Jesus" (Acts 9:28).

Through the rest of his earthly life Paul would be led through his deserts and oases, the sufferings and love of the soul's journey. "Suffering is part of your training; God is treating you as His sons [and daughters]" (Hebrews 12:7).

"We are in difficulties on all sides, but never cornered: we see no answer to our problems, but never despair: we have been persecuted, but never deserted: knocked down, but never killed: always, wherever we may be, we carry with us in our body the death of Jesus, so that the life of Jesus, too, may always be seen in our body . . . though this outer man of ours may be falling into decay, the inner man is renewed day by day. Yes, THE TROUBLES which are soon over, though they weigh little, TRAIN US FOR THE CARRYING OF A WEIGHT OF ETERNAL GLORY WHICH IS OUT OF ALL PROPORTION TO THEM" (2 Corinthians 4:8, 16).

"I have been crucified with Christ, and I live now not with my own life but with the life of Christ who lives in me" (Galatians 2:20).

In His glorified existence, Christ is beyond time in an "eternal now." His self-sacrifice was a perfect offering to the Father and all that is lacking is Christ physically present, in time, through the centuries. This is accomplished through the many humanities — male and female — that He spiritually prepares and transforms into His image. Through these countless humanities Christ is "incarnated" in every age, loving, working, suffering, dying and rising, triumphing over sin and death until the end of time as we know it.

"It makes me happy to suffer for you, as I am suffering now, and in my own body to do what I can to make up all that has still to be undergone by Christ for the sake of His body, the Church. I became the servant of the Church when God made me responsible for delivering God's message to you, the message which was a mystery hidden for generations and centuries and has now been revealed to His saints. . . . The mystery is Christ among you, your hope of glory. . . . It is for this I struggle wearily on, helped only by His power driving me irresistibly" (Colossians 1:24).

"O consuming Fire! Spirit of Love! descend within me and reproduce in me, as it were, an incarnation of the Word: that I may be to Him another humanity wherein He renews His mystery!" (Bl. Elizabeth of the Trinity, OCD).

Like Teresa of Avila, Paul experienced ecstasy, brought on by massive infusions of divine love. This activity of God within the soul purified and transformed it, bringing Paul to the state of spiritual marriage.

"I will move on to the visions and revelations I have had from the Lord. I know a man in Christ [Paul himself] who, fourteen years ago, was caught up — whether still in the body or out of the body, I do not know: God knows — right into the third heaven [highest heaven, in Teresa's terminology the seventh mansion where the Spiritual Marriage is consummated] . . . this person was caught up into paradise and heard things which must not and cannot be put into human language" (2 Corinthians 12:1).

Like the Apostles, St. Teresa of Avila and St. John of the Cross both received the grace of spiritual marriage during their earthly life.

"That which comes to pass in the union of the spiritual marriage is very different. The Lord appears in this center of the soul, not in an imaginative vision but in an intellectual one, although more delicate than those mentioned, as He appeared to the Apostles without entering through the door when He said to them 'Peace be with you.' What God communicates here to the soul in an instant is a secret so great and a favor so sublime — and the delight the soul experiences so extreme — that I don't know what to compare it to. . . . One can say no more — insofar as can be understood — than that the soul, I mean the spirit, is made one with God. . . . He has desired to be so joined with the creature that, just as those who are married cannot be separated, He doesn't want to be separated from the soul" (*The Interior Castle*, St. Teresa of Avila, VII, ch. 2:3).

"This spiritual marriage is incomparably greater than the spiritual espousal, for it is a total transformation in the Beloved in which each surrenders the entire possession of self to the other with a certain consummation of the union of love. The soul thereby becomes divine, becomes God through participation . . . the highest state attainable in this life. . . . The union wrought between the two natures and the communication of the divine to the human in this state is such that even though neither change their being, both appear to be God" (*Spiritual Canticle*, St. John of the Cross, ch. 22:3-4).

To reach this lofty state, St. John of the Cross reminds his readers, they must first undergo the dark night. The soul must be emptied before it can be filled.

"This dark night is an inflow of God into the soul, which purges it of its habitual ignorances and imperfections, natural and spiritual, and which the contemplatives call infused contemplation or mystical theology. Through this contemplation, God teaches the soul secretly and instructs it in the perfection of love without its doing anything nor understanding how this happens. Insofar as infused contemplation is loving wisdom of God, it produces two principal effects in the soul: it prepares the soul for the union with God through love by both purging and illumining it" (*The Dark Night*, St. John of the Cross, Bk. II, ch. 5:1).

"Dark contemplation brings the soul closer to God. . . . Because of his weakness, a person feels thick darkness and more profound obscurity the closer he comes to God, just as he would feel greater darkness and pain, because of the weakness and impurity of his eyes, the closer he approached the immense brilliance of the sun. The spiritual light is so bright and so transcendent that it blinds and darkens the natural intellect as it approaches" (*Ibid.*, Bk. II, ch. 16:11).

"A man would never have been able to accomplish this work himself, as we shall soon explain. Accordingly, God makes the soul die to all that He is not, so that when it is stripped and flayed of its old skin, He may clothe it anew. Its youth is renewed like the eagle's, clothed in the new man which is created, as the Apostle says, according to God. This renovation is: an illumination of the human intellect with supernatural light so that it becomes divine, united with the divine; an informing of the will with love of God so that it is no longer less than divine and loves in no other way than divinely. . . . And thus this soul will be a soul of heaven, heavenly and more divine than human" (*Ibid.*, ch. 13:11).

Every soul's love relationship with God is meant to reach completion in spiritual marriage in order to share the life of the Trinity in heaven. The Saints were brought to this sublime state by God while still on earth and visible to human eyes. The unusual mystical phenomena experienced by Teresa not only helped her to grow in love, but inspired her with the grace to communicate to her readers what God had worked in her soul. To the many witnesses of these events it was obvious that something supernatural was happening that was beyond their capacity to comprehend or explain — obviously the intervention of God.

Teresa lived in a time when it was generally believed that women "did not have the brains for mental prayer." It was also the time of the dreaded Inquisition, when any spiritual ideas or writings that became suspect frequently led to imprisonment or execution. Considering the mindset of the day, it is not surprising that divine intervention might be necessary to safeguard both Teresa and her writings.

"Once while wondering why I almost never had raptures in public any more, I heard: 'It's not necessary now; you have enough approval for what I intend' " (*Spiritual Testimonies*, St. Teresa of Avila, 9).

In the first of her writings, her *Life,* Teresa wrote with complete honesty about her spiritual experiences even though she did not, at the time, understand what she was going through. In spite of great fear and suffering she continued her journey in the dark night of faith, trusting completely in God. It was only in looking back and reflecting upon her experiences that Teresa was able to put them all into perspective. After her Spiritual Marriage, the "cloud of unknowing" was lifted, the spiritual "desert" had been crossed, and the "dark night" became brilliant in the light of infused divine wisdom. Teresa then wrote her inspired *Interior Castle,* for the spiritual benefit of all contemplative souls who would follow her along the "royal road."

"Insofar as I can understand the door of entry to this castle is prayer and reflection" *(Interior Castle,* St. Teresa of Avila, I, ch. 1:7).

Acquiring the habit of regular prayer is essential. One not only learns to pray by praying, but understanding increases. "What I want to explain to you is very difficult to understand without experience" *(Ibid.,* I, ch. 1:9). It should be realized that the activity of God and the stages of prayer cannot be neatly compartmentalized. Teresa uses the dwelling places as symbols to help express the inexpressible.

The first three rooms, or dwelling places, of the *Interior Castle* refer to the state of soul of most adults who believe in God, and are sincerely striving to lead a good life. The prayer of the souls in these three rooms would usually be "discursive meditation" or "acquired" contemplation, what Teresa called the "prayer of recollection." In her analogy of prayer and the four waters in her *Life,* Teresa described the prayer of beginners as "drawing water from the well," because of the effort it required. "Discursive work with the intellect is what is meant by fetching water from the well" *(Life,* St. Teresa of Avila, ch. 11:10).

These souls, Teresa explains, may find contemplative prayer demanding because of the hectic pace of everyday life. They find it difficult to "enter within themselves," because they are "so accustomed to being involved in external matters" *(Ibid.,* I, ch. 1:6).

Teresa confesses that the first twenty years of her own religious life were lived more on the surface than in the depths. "For some years, I was more anxious that the hour I had determined to spend in prayer be over than I was to remain there. . . . And I don't know what heavy penance could have come to mind that frequently I would not have gladly undertaken rather than recollect myself in the practice of prayer" *(Life,* St. Teresa of Avila, ch. 8:7).

A conversion experience involving a statue of Christ was considered by Teresa the turning point in her prayer life. The statue "represented the much wounded Christ . . . so that beholding it I was utterly distressed in seeing Him that way. . . . I felt so keenly aware of how poorly I thanked Him for those wounds that, it seems to me, my heart broke. Beseeching Him to strengthen me once and for all that I might not offend him, I threw myself down before Him with the greatest outpouring of tears. . . . I said that I would not rise from there until He granted what I was begging Him for. I believe certainly this was beneficial to me, because from that time I went on improving" *(Ibid.,* ch. 9:1-2).

In the *Interior Castle* the dividing line between natural and supernatural prayer is between the third and fourth dwelling places. It cannot be crossed without first sustaining a "crack" in that perfect image of ourselves that we cling to, a "metanoia" or "born-again" event which awakens the faculties of the soul. Through that crack, healing, divine light is able to penetrate. This is the light which guides the soul, but the soul must be willing to be led, willing to give up control in the spiritual area. A state of "spiritual childhood" is necessary for the soul after its "born-again" or conversion experience.

The transition from the third to the fourth dwelling place is probably the most difficult step for the soul, but it is the quantum leap to a new dimension. The spiritual world is entirely God's domain. We cannot demand the God-life, but must acquire the attitude and openness of soul necessary for His generous self-giving. In the natural world it is important for people to mature and become independent, self-controlled, efficient, and in charge of their lives. To humble oneself and admit the need of help is unthinkable for some persons. The experience of one's weakness and helplessness in the spiritual area is a far cry from reading about it or believing it conceptually.

This new awareness of one's spiritual condition is "knowing" with the soul's faculties, an interior knowing derived from experience. "The purest suffering brings with it the purest and most intimate knowing, and consequently the purest and highest joy, because it is a knowing from further within" (Spiritual Canticle, St. John of the Cross, St. 36:12). This is the self-knowledge that Teresa insists will be needed throughout the entire spiritual journey.

At each stage of the soul's descent within itself, it is like opening another sealed inner compartment which is then capable of being divinely illuminated after it has been cleaned and restored. The fire of divine love lights the way, urging the soul on to ever-greater depths and cauterizing the inner wounds as it proceeds. "Fire goes before Him and consumes His foes [our sins and faults]" (Psalm 97). The fire of love shames the soul into sorrow for past offenses and strengthens the determination to improve, the climate in which virtue thrives.

Not only is the darkness at each interior level experienced, it must be accepted as part of the self. For the individual in the first three rooms who has consciously tried to restrain or overcome bad habits, this darkness is unsettling. The person in this state has usually developed a pretty good opinion of himself or herself and now that image is being threatened, for it needs to be examined in a new light. Pride must be set aside for, Teresa said, "'Humility is

145

truth."

The area under our control, signified by the first three rooms, is only the tip of the iceberg. Bad habits may be kept in check by the individual, but the roots of these imperfections, which extend into the greater spiritual area, must also be eliminated. This is God's territory, and He alone does the work. "All the imperfections and disorders of the sensory part are rooted in the spirit and from it receive their strength" (*Dark Night*, St. John of the Cross, Bk. II, ch. 3:1).

Just as we cannot break down God's activity in the soul, the soul's journey, or its growth in prayer into separate entities, the human person is a composite whose various aspects are inseparable. Body, mind, and spirit can be divided only in human speech and thought. The areas of spirituality and psychology, especially, overlap and interact. I am not trained in psychology nor familiar with all of the technical terms, but must touch on some of these interacting areas, approaching them from the spiritual viewpoint.

Like parallel crystal shafts, the masculine/feminine facets of the soul extend into the inner depths. The two facets of the human spirit, which are naturally dark, correspond to the divine, which are all light. At each level the soul opens its "sealed compartments" to divine enlightenment. That which has been called the "dark" side of the soul is not so much "evil" as having the capacity for evil, being "primitive" or untaught (especially the anima/animus) and closed off from divine light. Choosing to act with free will and reason through these capacities would involve sin, just as temptation is not evil in itself, but only when accepted. Jesus, one with us in the divine/human spirit, experienced all the horror of the dark side of humanity and its sins "as if" He were guilty, and the consequences of that guilt, but He Himself had no personal guilt and was free from all sin.

It was helpful for me to picture the "anima," or less developed feminine side of the man, as his wild, spiritual "twin" who had been closed off from society, frustrated and rebellious, like the child Helen Keller, who had been imprisoned in herself beyond the reach of love, both human and divine, and unable to see, hear, or communicate with other human beings. (This would also be a more accurate representation of hell.) Through love, acceptance, and patient endurance the "other side of the soul's life" (Jung) can reach its fullest potential, and be integrated into the whole person. It is not accomplished overnight.

"Where there is no love, put love, and you will draw out love" (letter to Maria de la Encarnacion, St. John of the Cross).

For the woman it is the "animus" or masculine side of the soul that must be gradually developed and assimilated. I sympathize with the men, for it seems that by their very nature it is more difficult to admit and develop their feminine side and its gentle qualities than for women to accept and develop their masculine traits. But as long as men repress these attributes of God which are classified as feminine, they will never fully accept women as equals. They are depriving themselves by this attitude for their spiritual imbalance will be harmfully projected into their male/female relationships. As for their spiritual life, they will inhibit their souls' development by blocking this aspect of the divine inflow.

The ever-developing feminine side of the soul is apparent in the poems and commentaries of St. John of the Cross. The soul's attitude of surrender, which is called a feminine trait, is essential for divine union and spiritual marriage. "This spiritual marriage . . . is a total transformation in the Beloved in which each surrenders the entire possession of self to the other. . . . The soul thereby becomes divine . . . insofar as is possible in this life" (Spiritual Canticle, St. John of the Cross, St. 22:3).

Teresa begins her castle analogy by emphasizing the necessity for self-knowledge and humility throughout the entire spiritual journey.

"It is very important for any soul that practices prayer, whether little or much, not to hold itself back and stay in one corner. . . . Oh, but if it is in the room of self-knowl-edge! How necessary this room is — see that you under-stand me — even for those whom the Lord has brought into the very dwelling place where He abides. For never, however exalted the soul may be, is anything else fitting for it; nor could it be even were the soul to so desire. For humility, like the bee making honey in the beehive, is always at work. Without it, everything goes wrong. While we are on this earth nothing is more important to us than humility" (Interior Castle, St. Teresa of Avila, I, ch. 2:8-9).

Teresa advises souls not to become weighed down by concentrating on their own misery or sinfulness, but keep their spiritual gaze directed toward God. "Here it will discover its lowliness better than by thinking of itself" (Ibid., I, ch. 2:8). "In my opinion we shall never completely know ourselves if we don't strive to know God. By gazing at His grandeur, we get in touch with our own lowliness; by looking at His purity, we shall see our own filth; by pondering His humility, we shall see how far we are from being humble" (Ibid., I, ch. 2:9).

This paragraph points out the importance of the soul's attitude and intention in contemplative prayer. That which the soul lovingly gazes upon — God and His attributes — gradually becomes absorbed by the soul through that "crack" in its facade, which leaves it open and vulnerable to the divine infusions.

"Even though this is the first dwelling place, it is very rich and so precious that if the soul slips away from the vermin within it [faults], nothing will be left to do but ad-vance" (Ibid., I, ch. 2:11).

"Since in the first rooms souls are still absorbed in the world and engulfed in their pleasures and vanities, with their honors and pretenses, their vassals (which are the senses and faculties) don't have strength . . . and are easily conquered, even though they may go about with desires not to offend God and though they do perform good works. Those who see themselves in this state must approach His

Majesty as often as possible. . . . Truly, in all states it's necessary that strength come to us from God" (Ibid., I, ch. 2:12).

"If a person is to enter the second dwelling places, it is important that he strive to give up unnecessary things and business affairs. Each one should do this in conformity with his state in life" (Ibid., I, ch. 2:14).

Teresa writes that the second dwelling place "pertains to those who have already begun to practice prayer and have understood how important it is not to stay in the first dwelling places" (Ibid., II, ch. 1:2).

She describes the occasions for a possible conversion experience as "calls from the Lord." "These persons are able to hear the Lord when He calls. Since they are getting closer to where His Majesty dwells. . . . They come through words spoken by other good people, or through sermons, or through what is read in good books, or through the many things that are heard and by which God calls, or through illnesses and trials, or also THROUGH A TRUTH THAT HE TEACHES DURING THE BRIEF MOMENTS WE SPEND IN PRAYER; however lukewarm these moments may be, God esteems them highly. And you, Sisters, don't underestimate this first favor, nor should you become disconsolate if you don't respond at once to the Lord. His Majesty knows well how to wait many days and years, especially when He sees perseverance and good desires. This perseverance is most necessary here. One always gains much through perseverance" (Ibid., II, ch. 1:2-3).

"The whole aim of any person who is beginning prayer — and don't forget this, because it's very important — should be that he work and prepare himself with determination and every possible effort to bring his will into conformity with God's will. . . . THE GREATEST PERFECTION ATTAINABLE ALONG THE SPIRITUAL PATH LIES IN THIS CONFORMITY. . . . Don't think that in what concerns perfection there is some mystery or things unknown or still to be understood, for in perfect conformity to God's will lies all our good" (Ibid., II, ch. 1:8).

"If you should at times fall, don't become discouraged and stop striving to advance. For even from this fall God will draw out good. . . . I ask those who have not begun to enter within themselves to do so; and those who have begun, not to let the war [of the faculties] make them turn back. . . . IT IS FOOLISH TO THINK THAT WE WILL ENTER HEAVEN WITHOUT ENTERING INTO OURSELVES" (Ibid., II, ch. 1:9, 11).

Speaking of souls who enter the third dwelling places, Teresa says, "I believe that through the goodness of God there are many of these souls in the world. They long not to offend His Majesty, even guarding themselves against venial sins: they are fond of doing penance and setting aside periods for recollection; they spend their time well, practicing works of charity toward their neighbors: and are very balanced in their use of speech and dress and in the governing of their households — those who have them. Certainly, this is a state to be desired. And, in my opinion, there is no reason why entrance even into the final dwelling place should be denied these souls, nor will the Lord deny them this entrance if they desire it: for such a desire is an excellent way to prepare oneself so that every favor may be granted" (Ibid., III, ch. 1:5).

Teresa states that "it is not enough to say we want it" (ch. 1:6) for in this stage the individual is still in control. To enter the supernatural area of prayer the soul must respond to the "calls of the Lord," gradually give up the false self-image, admit the need for improvement, and endure the aridity of the desert. This brings alignment of wills. "There is no doubt that if a person perseveres in this nakedness and detachment from all worldly things he will reach his goal." The problem is, "We are fonder of consolations than we are of the cross" (Ibid., III, ch. 1:8-9).

"God often desires that His chosen ones feel their wretchedness, and He withdraws His favor a little. . . . This distress, I think, is a great mercy from God; and although it is a defect, it is very beneficial for humility" (Ibid., III, ch. 2:2).

"And believe me the whole affair doesn't lie in whether or not we wear the religious habit but in striving to practice the virtues, in surrendering our will to God in everything, in bringing our life into accordance with what His Majesty ordains for it, and in desiring that His will, not ours, be done" (Ibid., III, ch. 2:6).

Of the fourth dwelling place Teresa says, "I have greatly enlarged upon this because IT IS THE ONE WHICH MORE SOULS ENTER," and that "THE NATURAL AND SUPERNATURAL ARE JOINED IN IT" (Ibid., IV, 3:14). This is the reason for the new way of proceeding. God "meets" the soul at the entry into the land of spirit, and takes it by the hand like a little child. John of the Cross calls the soul in this stage "a blind man." The soul's affections and appetites have been lured away from mere earthly pleasures through the soul's enjoyment of spiritual consolations. But it takes a little time to acquire a taste for the "manna," as spiritual food is more subtle and delicate. Through determination, strengthened by the initial absorbing of divine love, the soul will develop a new way of seeing, loving, thinking, and acting, more divine than human.

"Supernatural experiences begin here. These are something most difficult to explain" (Ibid., IV, 1:1).

"It will seem that to reach these dwelling places one will have had to live in the others a long while. Although it is usual that a person will have to have stayed in those already spoken about, there is no certain rule. . . . For the Lord gives when He desires, as He desires, and to whom He desires. Since these blessings belong to Him, He does no injustice to anyone" (Ibid., IV, 1:2).

Infused prayer begins in the fourth dwelling place and for the majority of the spiritual children God's loving wisdom will be infused drop by drop, as the false self is progressively stripped away. Spiritual growth is a matter of "becoming," not how much the soul feels or comprehends with the intellect. Teresa teaches the soul what it must do.

"In order to profit by this path and ascend to the dwelling places we desire, THE IMPORTANT THING IS NOT TO THINK MUCH BUT TO LOVE MUCH; AND SO DO THAT WHICH BEST STIRS YOU TO LOVE. Perhaps we don't know what love is. I wouldn't be very surprised, because it doesn't consist in great delight but in desiring with strong determination to please God in everything. . . . These are the signs of love. Don't think the matter lies in thinking of nothing else, and that if you become a little distracted all is lost" (Ibid., IV, 1:7).

The love relationship continues even if the intellect is occupied, and distractions will always be a part of the human condition. The important thing is not to become overly upset by them.

"Ordinarily the mind flies about quickly, for only God can hold it fast in such a way as to make it seem that we are somehow loosed from this body. I have seen, I think, that the faculties of my soul were occupied and recollected in God while my mind on the other hand was distracted. This distraction puzzled me. . . . But the soul is perhaps completely joined with Him in the dwelling places very close to the center while the mind is on the outskirts of the castle suffering from a thousand wild and poisonous beasts, and MERITING BY THIS SUFFERING. As a result we should not be disturbed: nor should we abandon prayer. . . . For the most part, all the trials and disturbances come from our not understanding ourselves. . . .

"Even in this life, the Lord frees the soul from these miseries when it reaches the last dwelling place" (Ibid., IV, ch. 1:8-9, 12).

Teresa calls the beginnings of infused prayer of the fourth dwelling place "the prayer of quiet." In some of her other writings Teresa also describes a deeper recollection as "prayer of quiet," which points up the difficulty of trying to isolate and analyze spiritual experiences. As divine love grows in the soul, infused prayer has an ever-deepening quality. It is more important that the soul is open and grateful to receive the love, than that it be labeled. Sometimes the Lord will give a brief foretaste of supernatural prayer to beginners, "in order to invite souls by the sight of what takes place in the remaining dwelling places and so that they will prepare themselves to enter them" (Ibid., III, ch. 2:9). But the transition from what we can do ourselves, to what is beyond our control, is what Teresa represents as the fourth dwelling places.

In her *Life*, Teresa calls water obtained by a water wheel and aqueducts the "second water," which represented the "prayer of quiet" or the beginning of infused prayer. The "third water" or "sleep of the faculties" was described as "a river or spring," which might be preparatory touches of union, not yet permanent union. Regarding the nature of union, Teresa writes, "There are various degrees of intensity" (*Interior Castle*, V, ch. 2:1). In the *Interior Castle* Teresa also explains, "It is possible that in dealing with these interior matters I might contradict something of what I said elsewhere. That's no surprise, because in the almost fifteen years since I wrote it, the Lord may perhaps have given me clearer understanding in these matters than I had before" (*Ibid.*, IV, ch. 2:7).

In the fourth dwelling place Teresa enlarges upon these symbols, and describes "two founts with two water troughs." "These two troughs are filled with water in different ways: with one the water comes from far away through many aqueducts and the use of much ingenuity: with the other the source of the water is right there, and the trough fills without any noise . . . the water overflows once the trough is filled, forming a large stream. There is no need of any skill, nor does the building of aqueducts have to continue; but water is always flowing from the spring. The water coming from the aqueducts is comparable, in my opinion, to the consolations I mentioned that are drawn from meditation. . . . With this other fount, the water comes from its own source which is God" (*Ibid.*, IV, ch. 2:2-4).

Teresa seems to be describing what the soul might experience at the transition from its discursive meditation, and acquired contemplation or recollected prayer, which it prepares for and initiates, to the infused prayer of quiet which God instills in the soul. Through the first type, the soul hovers on the borderline between natural and supernatural prayer, perhaps experiencing foretastes or glimpses. God must bring the soul across, but without that initial preparation, it would not even be at the border. The first prayer begins in ourselves (senses and faculties) and ends in God; the second "begins in God and ends in ourselves" (Ibid., IV, ch. 2:4) as the delight overflows from the spirit and is enjoyed by the senses and faculties.

Teresa states that the experience is not from the heart but "from another part still more interior, as from something deep. I think this must be the center of the soul" (Ibid., IV, ch. 2:5), and that the infusion of divine love enlarges the capacity for love.

"What I think is helpful . . . for explaining this matter is the idea of expansion. It seems that since that heavenly water begins to rise from this spring I'm mentioning that is deep within us, it swells and expands our whole interior being, producing ineffable blessings: nor does the soul even understand what is given to it there. It perceives a fragrance, let us say for now, as though there were in that interior depth a brazier giving off sweet-smelling perfumes. No light is seen, nor is the place seen where the brazier is: but the warmth and the fragrant fumes spread through the entire soul and even often enough, as I have said, the body shares in them. See now that you understand me; no heat is felt, nor is there the scent of any perfume, for the experience is more delicate than an experience of these things; but I use the examples only so as to explain it to you" (Ibid., IV, ch. 2:6).

"This spiritual delight is not something that can be imagined, because however diligent our efforts we cannot acquire it. The very experience of it makes us realize that it is not of the same metal as we ourselves but fashioned from the purest gold of the divine wisdom. Here, in my opinion, the faculties are not united but absorbed and looking as though in wonder at what they see" (Ibid., IV, ch. 2:6).

At every stage, Teresa reminds her readers, it is not the consolations and favors that determine the soul's authentic spiritual growth, but the loving acts going out to its neighbors, for the nature of love is to serve. "I came to serve, not to be served." The increasing divine love has a purpose, to help heal and transform the world through individuals as instruments.

"The will must in some way be united with God's will. But it is in the effects and deeds following afterward that one discerns the true value of prayer; there is no better crucible for testing prayer" (Ibid., IV, ch. 2:8).

Teresa advises souls not to become too concerned with "measuring" or evaluating their progress, since it is in God's hands. This process directs attention back to "self," when we should "forget ourselves and our own profit and comfort and delight." "Leave the soul in God's hands, let Him do whatever He wants with it, with the greatest disinterest about your own benefit as is possible and the greatest resignation to the will of God" (Ibid., IV, ch. 3:6).

Love, which resides in the will, is able to unite with God before the intellect and memory are completely purified. Until they are purified and fully enlightened, the intellect will not comprehend all that is being absorbed and stored. When the faculties are not suspended by God the intellect may roam, for it is used to proceeding by way of reasoning and, when not functioning, it is like a bored child whose attention is not being occupied.

"It is good to be aware that one is in God's presence and of who God is. If what it feels within itself absorbs it, well and good. But let it not strive to understand the nature of this recollection, for it is given to the will. Let the soul enjoy it without any endeavors other than some loving words.

"The will has such deep rest in its God that the clamor of the intellect is a terrible bother to it. There is no need to pay any attention to this clamor, for doing so would make the will lose much of what it enjoys. But one should leave the intellect go and surrender oneself into the arms of love" (Ibid., IV, ch. 3:7-8).

Teresa points out some of the effects of the ever-increasing love relationship. "The soul is not as tied down as it was before in things pertaining to the service of God, but has much more freedom . . . not constrained by fear of hell . . . this soul is left with great confidence that it will enjoy Him." There is no fear of "doing penance and losing its health . . . or of trials. Its faith is more alive; it knows that if it suffers trials for God, His Majesty will give it the grace to suffer them with patience. . . . In sum, there is an improvement in all the virtues" (Ibid., IV, ch. 3:9).

In the fifth dwelling place the prayer of union is experienced. In her *Life,* Teresa called it the "fourth water." In the *Interior Castle* Teresa also compares it to the "inner wine cellar" of the bride in the Song of Songs. The complete surrender of the will, which started with little things and has been required at every step of the way, has been completed.

"I understand this union to be the wine cellar where the Lord wishes to place us when He desires and as He desires. But however great the effort we make to do so, we cannot enter. His Majesty must place us there and enter Himself into the center of our soul. And . . . He doesn't want our will to have any part to play, for it has been entirely surrendered to Him. Neither does He want the door of the faculties and of the senses to be opened, for they are all asleep. But He wants to enter the center of the soul without going through any door, as He entered the place where His disciples were when He said, pax vobis, or as He left the tomb without lifting away the stone. Further on you will see in the last dwelling place how His Majesty desires that the soul enjoy Him in its own center even much more than here" (*Ibid.*, V, ch. 1:12).

Teresa offers encouragement to all prayerful souls: "There are indeed only a few who fail to enter this dwelling place. . . . There are various degrees, and for that reason I say that MOST enter these places. But I believe that only a few will experience some of the things that I will say are in this room. Yet even if souls do no more than reach the door, God is being very merciful to them" (*Ibid.*, V, ch. 1:2).

Every soul has the potential to receive this "precious pearl of contemplation. . . . Yet few of us dispose ourselves that the Lord may communicate it to us. . . . Since in some way we can enjoy heaven on earth, be brave in begging the Lord to give us His grace in such a way that nothing will be lacking through our own fault; that He show us the way and strengthen the soul that it may dig until it finds this hidden treasure. THE TRUTH IS THAT THE TREASURE LIES WITHIN OUR VERY SELVES" (*Ibid.*, V, ch. 1:2).

Teresa describes her experience of union. Her description helps to clarify the infusion of mystical love and knowledge as it bypasses the created intellect and senses: "God has made this soul a fool with regard to all so as better to impress upon it true wisdom. For during the time of this union it neither sees, nor hears, nor understands, because the union is always short and seems to the soul even much shorter than it probably is. God so places Himself in the interior of that soul that when it returns to itself it can in no way doubt that it was in God and God was in it. This truth remains with it so firmly that even though years go by without God's granting that favor again, the soul can neither forget nor doubt that it was in God and God was in it. This certitude is what matters now.

"Now, you will ask me, how did the soul see this truth or understand if it didn't see or understand anything? I don't say that it then saw the truth but that afterward it sees the truth clearly, not because of a vision but because of a certitude remaining in the soul that only God can place there" (*Ibid.,* V, ch. 1:9-10).

In the fifth dwelling place Teresa uses the analogy of the silkworm that is transformed into a butterfly as a symbol of the transformed soul. "This silkworm starts to live . . . by the heat of the Holy Spirit." It grows through "help given to us all by God . . . the Church . . . confession, reading good books, and hearing sermons . . . and by good meditations until it is grown. Its being grown is what is relevant to what I'm saying."

For then, Teresa writes, "It begins to spin the silk and build the house wherein it will die. I would like to point out here that this house is Christ . . . our life is hidden in Christ," and the soul begins to "weave this little cocoon by getting rid of our self-love and self-will. When the soul is, in this prayer, dead to the world, a little white butterfly comes forth. Oh greatness of God! How transformed the soul is when it comes out of this prayer after having been placed within the greatness of God and so closely joined with Him for a little while. . . . Truly, I tell you that the soul doesn't recognize itself" (*Ibid.,* V, ch. 2:2-3, 6-7).

"It no longer has any esteem for the works it did while a worm, which was to weave the cocoon little by little: it now has wings. . . . It doesn't wonder as much at what the saints suffered now that it understands through experience how the Lord helps and transforms a soul, for it doesn't recognize itself or its image" (*Ibid.,* V, ch. 2:8).

Teresa cautions, "In one way or another, there must be a cross while we live," but "I don't mean to say that those who arrive here do not have peace; they do have it, and it is very deep" (*Ibid.,* V, ch. 2:9-10).

Teresa insists that extraordinary spiritual experiences are not necessary for union, only conformity with God's will. "Since so much gain comes from entering this place, it will be good to avoid giving the impression that those to whom the Lord doesn't give things that are so supernatural are left without hope. True union can very well be reached, with God's help, if we make the effort to obtain it by keeping our wills fixed only on that which is God's will" (Ibid., V, ch. 3:3).

"The Lord asks of us only two things: love of His Majesty and love of our neighbor. These are what we must work for. By observing them with perfection, we do His will and so will be united with Him. . . . If we practice love of neighbor with great perfection, we will have done everything. . . . We will not reach perfection in the love of neighbor if that love doesn't rise from love of God as its root" (Ibid., V, ch. 3:7, 9).

The sixth dwelling place is the place of the spiritual betrothal. Teresa experienced intense suffering, both spiritual and physical, before receiving the grace of spiritual marriage. "Oh, God help me, what interior and exterior trials the soul suffers before entering the seventh dwelling place!" (Ibid., VI, ch. 1:1).

Teresa had to experience the dark emptiness at every level of her inner depths, in order to open these areas to the divine light. "This torment comes from above, and earthly things are of no avail in the matter. Our great God wants us to know our own misery and that He is king; and this is very important for what lies ahead" (Ibid., VI, ch. 1:12).

"Courage is necessary for this knowledge and for the many other graces given to the soul the Lord has brought to this stage" (Ibid., VI, ch. 5:6).

The virtues, especially humility, are strengthened; "The soul sees clearly that if it has anything good this is given by God and is by no means its own" (Ibid., VI, ch. 1:4). "This action of love is so powerful that the soul dissolves with desire" (Ibid., VI, ch. 2:4).

Teresa experienced massive divine infusions which caused rapture. "The spirit truly seems to go forth from the body. On the other hand, it is clear that this person is not dead; at least, he cannot say whether for some moments he was in the body or not. It seems to him that he was entirely in another region different from this in which we live, where there is shown another light so different from earth's light that if he were to spend his whole life trying to imagine that light, along with the other things, he would be unable to do so. It happens that within an instant so many things together are taught him that if he were to work for many years with his imagination and mind in order to systematize them he wouldn't be able to do so. . . . The eyes of the soul see much better than do we with bodily eyes here on earth, and without words understanding of some things is given" (*Ibid.*, VI, ch. 5:7).

The wounds of love, raptures, and locutions are all gradual preparations, ways of adorning the soul with God's own splendor so that He can unite it to Himself as His equal. Teresa describes her experience of the spiritual marriage, but each soul will have its own unique journey. "Each one of us has a soul, but since we do not prize souls as is deserved by creatures made in the image of God, we do not understand the deep secrets that lie in them" (*Ibid.*, VII, ch. 1:1).

The seventh dwelling place is "another heaven" where "He dwells alone" (*Ibid.*, VII, ch. 1:3). "Now then, when His Majesty is pleased to grant the soul this divine marriage that was mentioned, He first brings it into His own dwelling place. He desires that the favor be different from what it was at other times when He gave the soul raptures. I really believe that in rapture He unites it with Himself, as well as in the prayer of union that was mentioned. But it doesn't seem to the soul that it is called to enter into its center, as it is here in this dwelling place. . . . These things matter little; whether the experience comes in one way or another, the Lord joins the soul to Himself. . . . In this seventh dwelling place . . . our good God now desires to remove the scales from the soul's eyes and let it see and understand, although in a strange way, something of the favor He grants it . . . the Most Blessed Trinity, all three Persons, through an intellectual vision, is revealed to it through a certain representation of the truth" (*Ibid.*, VII, ch. 1:3, 5-6).

God shares not only His love but His wisdom with the bride/soul. As St. John of the Cross wrote, "The possessions of both are held in common."

Teresa once described the divine touches and infusions in contemplation as being like the fire of two candles that flame together for a time, then separate. After spiritual marriage the two flames are one, nevermore to part. "O my soul, what a wonderful battle you have waged in this pain, and how literally true is what happens here! Since 'my Beloved is for me and I for my Beloved,' who will be able to separate and extinguish two fires so enkindled? It would amount to laboring in vain, for the two fires have become one" (*Soliloquies*, XVI:4, St. Teresa of Avila, Collected Works, Vol. 1).

Contemplative prayer provides the rendezvous for the soul to be alone with its God, as the two in their sameness rest in wordless communication. In the deep stages of contemplation, when our bride/soul unites as one with its Source we experience, in and with God, His existence beyond time, a foretaste of our heavenly existence. That which we sense but briefly during our time-oriented earthly lives will be enjoyed as a permanent state in heaven.

"So in this temple of God, in this His dwelling place, He alone and the soul rejoice together in the deepest silence" (*Interior Castle*, St. Teresa of Avila, VII, ch. 3:11).

The bride/soul is all eyes in its loving gaze, all peace in echoing stillness, all joy in infinite oneness, and all light in its answering fire.

The "Be"-ing of God, beyond time, does not translate into verbal language, although the vibrant presence of the Indwelling Trinity is experienced with certitude. It calls forth a sympathetic vibration from the deepest part of the self. The tremors are perceived but indescribable: a Touch of Love which quivers the heartstrings; Spirit-Wings which overshadow the soul; the Breeze of the Spirit which troubles the waters; the Fiery Glow which lures the soul on; for touched by the Spark it longed for the Flame, and in

161

the spiritual marriage has itself become a Living Flame of Love. Searching hearts draw near to this radiance.

"Through those who approach Me I will manifest My sacredness" (Leviticus 10:3).

The Divine Immensity overflows in all directions, lives are mended, souls are healed and made new. The fire that Jesus so desired to spread is not the nuclear fire that so many fear, but the transforming fire of love.

"My dear people, you must not think it unaccountable that you should be tested by fire. There is nothing extraordinary in what has happened to you . . . it means that you have the Spirit of glory, the Spirit of God resting on you" (1 Peter 4:12, 15).

We are already assured of the victory: "I am making the whole of creation new. . . . It is already done" (Revelation 21:5-6). Somewhere in the future, at a time known but to God, the "new Jerusalem" is waiting. The natural world and the supernatural will mesh as God takes the world/soul, like a bride, into the Trinitarian embrace. As is the case with the individual soul, if the world/soul is spiritually prepared it will be a gentle, loving embrace.

"Let us be glad and joyful and give praise to God, because this is the time for the marriage of the Lamb. His bride is ready, and she has been able to dress herself in dazzling white linen, because her linen is made of the good deeds of the saints. . . . Happy are those who are invited to the wedding feast" (Revelation 19:7).

"For Yahweh is creating something new on earth: the Woman sets out to find her Husband again" (Jeremiah 31:22).

Individually and collectively we are steadily moving through time to that "day" and "hour." Whether that ultimate day comes within our lifetime or not, we are all involved in its unfolding. The "new Jerusalem" is a spiritual kingdom, and each one of us has a stone (transformed soul) to contribute. Jesus is the "keystone" and the "twelve foundation stones . . . bore the name of one of the twelve Apostles" (Revelation 21:14).

Each soul transformed in God, or on its way, inevitably brings the world closer to its completion, like single tiny candle flames multiplying to dispel the darkness. As "carriers" and "lamps" souls just have to be available and willing. Many souls will be called upon to do more, but this much everyone can do. It is the most valuable inheritance we can leave for our children and all humanity — our sisters and brothers.

"I will tell you something that has been secret: that we are not all going to die, but we shall all be changed. This will be instantaneous, in the twinkling of an eye, when the last trumpet sounds. It will sound and the dead will be raised, imperishable, and we shall be changed as well, because our present perishable nature must put on imperishability and this mortal nature must put on immortality. When this perishable nature has put on imperishability, and when this mortal nature has put on immortality, then the words of Scripture will come true: Death is swallowed up in victory. Death, where is your victory? Death, where is your sting? . . . So let us thank God for giving us the victory through our Lord Jesus Christ" (1 Corinthians 15:51).

If we look back and reflect upon our spiritual history, we find that God has been constantly encouraging His children to partake of the Living Waters and the transforming Fire of Love, eager to divinize the soul who would respond.

"He has set fire and water before you; put out your hand to whichever you prefer" (Sirach 15:16).

"Oh, come to the water all you who are thirsty; though you have no money, come!" (Isaiah 55:1). "Yahweh will always guide you, giving you relief in desert places . . . and you shall be like a watered garden, like a spring of water whose waters never run dry" (Isaiah 58:11).

"Love is strong as death, the flash of it is a flash of fire, a flame of Yahweh Himself" (Song of Songs 8:6).

"You tested us, God, You refined us like silver . . . but

now the ordeal by fire and water is over, and You allow us once more to draw breath" (Psalm 66).

"Now towards her I send flowing peace, like a river. . . . At the sight your heart will rejoice" (Isaiah 66:12, 14).

To become Living Flames of Love we must feed the fire so that it does not die — with contemplative prayer. To drink of the Living Waters we must descend into our depths — in contemplative prayer. Divine intimacy, through contemplation, is as old as mankind itself, although in modern times the contemplative side of nature is often overlooked. As an eagle hovers over its nest inciting its young to fly, the Spirit hovers over the dark "abyss" of the soul inciting it to soar to God.

Contemplation is not only an important part of Christianity, but it goes back to our Judaeo-Christian roots. The Hebrew word describing God "resting" on the Sabbath has connotations of just breathing, existing, or "Be"-ing ("I Am Who Am"). Life was difficult in ancient times, especially for the average person without servants, and there was not much time for leisure. Sabbath laws were meant to ensure a regular time for doing nothing, a cessation of activity, freedom to "waste time" with God in wordless communion. The principle of the Sabbath was that forbidden by law from working, and restricted in physical movement, people would learn how to just "be" in the presence of God. "Be still and know [experience] that I am God" (Psalm 46:10). Over the years, as is so often the case with human nature, the rules increased in number and importance to the point where they often obscured the original intent and purpose of the Sabbath.

Once the basic process of spiritual development is discerned, we can recognize similar accounts in Scripture. People have often wondered why God seemed more personally involved with the men and women of Bible times than He is today, but God is the same "yesterday, today, and tomorrow," and so are human beings. What we read in the Bible are experiences and events described by souls

164

in the various stages of the spiritual journey. With the clearer perception of their spiritual faculties they were able to "see" God always at work in the world beneath ordinary surface appearances.

As they travel through their actual or spiritual deserts and dark nights, the holy people of the Bible cry out to God in their spiritual hunger and thirst. It is the eternal cry of the loving soul seeking its Beloved. They complain of their suffering and the seeming "absence" of God during the purifying times, and sing with joy as God infuses His mystical love and knowledge in the betrothal or bridal states.

"O God, You are my God, for You I long; for You my soul is thirsting. My body pines for You like a dry, weary land without water" (Psalm 63:2).

"That heavy hand of His drags groans from me. If only I knew how to reach Him. . . . Let Him test me in the crucible: I shall come out pure gold" (Job 23:2, 10).

"My flesh and my heart are pining with love" (Psalm 73:26).

"My heart has said of You, 'Seek His face' " (Psalm 30:7).

"I remember, and my soul melts within me. . . . Deep is calling to deep" (Psalm 42:4, 7).

"After my awaking, He will set me close to Him, and from my flesh I shall look on God" (Job 19:26).

"How precious, God, Your love! Hence the sons of men take shelter in the shadow of Your wings. . . . You give them drink from Your river of pleasure; yes, with You is the fountain of life, by Your light we see the light" (Psalm 36:7).

"In my inmost being You teach me wisdom" (Psalm 50).

"Come, let us return to Yahweh, He has torn us to pieces, but He will heal us . . . on the third day He will raise us and we shall live in His presence" (Hosea 6:1).

"You shall be called 'My Delight' and your land 'The

Wedded,' for Yahweh takes delight in you and your land will have its wedding. Like a young man marrying a virgin, so will the One Who built you wed you, and as the bridegroom rejoices in his bride, so will your God rejoice in you" (Isaiah 62:4).

The most complete allegorical description of the spiritual journey in the Old Testament is the Song of Songs. At the end of the poem there is a conversation among the Persons of the Trinity. They are asking what they shall do for their "sister" on the day of her betrothal. They are speaking of the soul — the soul is the "sister" of God, of His very essence.

"Our sister is little and she has no breasts as yet. [The soul is not yet spiritually mature.] What shall we do for our sister when her courtship begins? If she is a wall, we will build upon it a silver parapet: if she is a door, we will reinforce it with a cedar plank" (Song of Songs 8:8). When the spiritual courtship begins, God Himself will reinforce and fortify the soul through the divine infusions, making it strong enough to endure the intensity of union and spiritual marriage.

The Song begins with the enamored soul, who has tasted spiritual delights, seeking a deeper, more permanent relationship. "Draw me in Your footsteps. . . . The King has brought me into His rooms. . . . We shall praise Your love above wine; how right it is to love You" (Ibid., 1:4).

"I am dark but beautiful" (Ibid., 1:5), dark because the soul is not yet divinely enlightened, but beautiful because the soul is the sister or essence of God. There is a need for an initial effort on the part of the bride/soul, and she goes in search of her love. There are sufferings brought on by God's seeming absence — "My soul failed at His flight, I sought Him but I did not find Him" (Ibid., 5:6) — and moments of tenderness as the soul experiences the touches of divine love — "I found Him Whom my heart loves. I held Him fast, nor would I let Him go" (Ibid., 3:4).

God lets the soul know of His love — "You are wholly

beautiful, My love, and without a blemish" — for the soul has endured the necessary purification. "You ravish My heart, My sister, My promised bride. . . . She is a garden enclosed, my sister, my promised bride; a garden enclosed, a sealed fountain" (Ibid., 4:7, 9, 12). The deepest part of the soul is reserved for God alone, a "garden enclosed." Carmel means "garden," and to "walk with God in the garden" is a symbol of contemplation. The bride/soul responds, "Let my Beloved come into His garden, let Him taste its rarest fruits," virtues that God Himself has imparted to the soul, and of which the soul is now aware.

Beloved souls are encouraged to enjoy in contemplation the delights and fruits of their love and intimate union. (Bridegroom) "Eat, friends, and drink, drink deep, my dearest friends." (Bride) "I sleep, but my heart is awake. I hear my Beloved knocking" (Ibid., 5:1-2). Now the intellect, imagination, and memory are stilled in this "sleep of contemplation," while the heart (love/will) "watches" or gazes on God. Across the abyss of eternity God and the soul gaze at each other and are lost in love. Who can know the depths and intensity of divine love? None but these two, the soul and its God. Being divine, God can love only in a divine manner, and desires a soul capable of an answering fire.

"My Beloved is mine and I am His" (Ibid., 6:3). The bride/soul experiences the grace of spiritual marriage and is adorned with God's own splendor. "Who is this that comes forth like the dawn, as beautiful as the moon, as resplendent as the sun, as awe-inspiring as bannered troops?" (Ibid., 6:10).

Similar experiences are described in Psalm 44: "So shall the King desire your beauty. . . . All glorious is the King's daughter [soul] as she enters; her raiment is threaded with spun gold. In embroidered apparel she is borne in to the King . . . they enter the palace of the King" (Ibid., 44:12, 14, 16).

In his Spiritual Canticle, fashioned after the Song of Songs, John of the Cross explains the difficulty that exists in trying to explain spiritual matters. "It would be foolish to think that expressions of love arising from mystical understanding, like these stanzas, are fully explainable. The Spirit of the Lord, who abides in us and aids our weakness, as St. Paul says (Romans 8:26), pleads for us with unspeakable groanings in order to manifest what we can neither fully understand nor comprehend.

"Who can describe the understanding He gives to loving souls in whom He dwells? And who can express the experience He imparts to them? Who, finally, can explain the desires He gives them? Certainly, no one can! Not even they who receive these communications. As a result these persons let something of their experiences overflow in figures and similes, and from the abundance of their spirit pour out secrets and mysteries rather than rational explanations" (*Spiritual Canticle*, St. John of the Cross).

"These stanzas, then, were composed in a love flowing from abundant mystical understanding. . . . For mystical wisdom, which comes through love and is the subject of these stanzas, NEED NOT BE UNDERSTOOD DISTINCTLY IN ORDER TO CAUSE LOVE AND AFFECTION IN THE SOUL, FOR IT IS GIVEN ACCORDING TO THE MODE OF FAITH, THROUGH WHICH WE LOVE GOD WITHOUT UNDERSTANDING HIM" (*Ibid.*, Prologue).

Although there are basic stages or "levels" of the spiritual journey at which every soul will eventually arrive, the "steps" ascending to these levels may not be experienced in the manner that St. John of the Cross describes. In his *Spiritual Canticle* the more intense "touches of love" which cause the bride/soul to overflow with loving words are followed by a "moaning" or sense of God's "absence," increasing the soul's desire and urging it onward to the next "step" in which God's loving presence is again experienced. This back-and-forth movement corresponds to the seeming absence of God in the "desert," followed by the delight and consolation of the "oasis."

The first thirteen stanzas of John's *Spiritual Canticle*

describe the soul searching for her Beloved, enduring the emptying and filling of the desert journey. Commitment of the will is necessary, not just once, but at every step of the way. The spiritual betrothal between God and the soul takes place in the fourteenth and fifteenth stanzas. In stanza 22 the perfected soul is brought to the state of Spiritual Marriage.

John of the Cross reaffirms the spiritual principle that Teresa insisted upon: "In mystical theology which is known through love . . . one not only knows but at the same time experiences" (Ibid., Prologue). Throughout the stanzas John describes these experiences through poetic imagery, and often refers to the Songs: "He calls the soul His crown, His bride, and the joy of His heart, and He takes her now in His arms and goes forth with her as the bridegroom from his bridal chamber." John then proceeds with his poetic version of spiritual marriage. "The bride has entered the sweet garden of her desire, And she rests in delight, Laying her neck on the gentle arms of her Beloved" (Ibid., St. 22:1).

"Here the Bridegroom speaks and, in calling the soul 'bride,' declares two things: First He tells how, now victorious, she has reached this pleasant state of spiritual marriage, which was His as well as her ardent longing.

"And second, He enumerates the properties of this state which the soul now enjoys, such as: resting in delight and laying her neck on the gentle arms of her Beloved" (Spiritual Canticle, St. John of the Cross, St. 22:2).

"It should be noted that before the soul reaches this state she first exercises herself both in the trials and the bitterness of mortification [deserts and dark nights] and in meditation on spiritual things. . . . Afterwards she embarks upon the CONTEMPLATIVE WAY. Here she passes along the paths and straits of love . . . where the spiritual espousal is wrought . . . she advances along the unitive way [divine union, surrender of will], in which she receives many remarkable communications, visits, gifts, and jewels from her Bridegroom [adornments of God's splendor] and as one betrothed, learns of her Beloved and BECOMES PERFECT IN LOVING HIM"

(Ibid., St. 22:3).

The verse that begins "The bride has entered" is "Where the spiritual marriage between this soul and the Son of God is effected. This spiritual marriage is incomparably greater than the spiritual espousal, for it is a total transformation in the Beloved. . . . The soul thereby becomes divine, becomes God through participation . . . the highest state attainable in this life. Just as in the consummation of carnal marriage there are two in one flesh . . . when the spiritual marriage between God and the soul is consummated, there are two natures in one spirit and love, as St. Paul says in making this same comparison: 'He who is joined to the Lord is one spirit with Him' " *(Ibid.,* St. 22:3).

"She has been transformed into her God, here referred to as 'the sweet garden.' . . . The union wrought between the two natures and the communication of the divine to the human in this state is such that EVEN THOUGH NEITHER CHANGE THEIR BEING, BOTH APPEAR TO BE GOD" *(Ibid.,* St. 22:4).

As the soul becomes more and more God-like it does not lose its individual identity, for grace builds upon nature and perfects it. St. Paul was still Paul, reflecting his unique Spirit of Christ and living it differently than Mary, Peter, James, John, or, at a later time, Teresa of Avila and John of the Cross, and the other Saints throughout the ages.

Transformed souls are meant to effect changes on earth. "I have prayed for you, Simon, that your faith may not fail, and once you have recovered, you in your turn must strengthen your brothers [and sisters]" (Luke 22:32). Humanity is at its best, most God-like, when it reaches out in compassion to others through the Spirit of Christ.

John of the Cross declares that the soul that has attained spiritual marriage "lives in this state a life as happy and glorious as is God's, let each one consider here, if he can, how pleasant her life is; just as God is incapable of feeling any distaste neither does she feel any, for the delight of God's glory is experienced and enjoyed in the substance of the soul now transformed in Him" *(Ibid.,* St. 22:5).

" 'And she rests in delight, laying her neck.' The 'neck' refers here to the soul's strength by means of which, as we said, is effected this union with her Bridegroom: because SHE WOULD BE UNABLE TO ENDURE SO INTIMATE AN EMBRACE IF SHE WERE NOT NOW VERY STRONG. And because the soul labored by means of this strength, practiced the virtues, and conquered, it is right that with the strength by which she struggled and conquered she repose, laying her neck 'on the gentle arms of her Beloved' " *(Ibid.,* St. 22:6).

"To recline her neck on the arms of God is to have her strength, or, better, her weakness, now united to the strength of God, for the 'arms' signify God's strength . . . for NOW GOD IS THE SOUL'S STRENGTH AND SWEETNESS, in which she is sheltered and protected against all evils, and habituated to the delight of all goods" *(Ibid.,* St. 22:6-7).

John writes that when the bride in the Songs calls God her "brother," "she indicates the equality of love between the two in the espousal before this state is reached" *(Ibid.,* St. 22:7).

All baptized souls are united to Christ, John of the Cross points out, but the spiritual marriage deals with the soul's gradual development until it reaches the divine perfection it was created for: "to know, love, and serve God, and be happy with Him forever in heaven." This answer, that children have rattled off by rote, pertains to the experiential knowing, loving, and serving of the transformed soul.

"The espousal made on the Cross is not the one we now speak of. For that espousal is accomplished immediately when God gives the first grace, which is bestowed on each one at Baptism. The espousal of which we speak bears reference to perfection and IS NOT ACHIEVED SAVE GRADUALLY AND BY STAGES . . . one is attained at the soul's pace, and thus little by little, and the other [Baptism] at God's pace, and thus immediately" *(Ibid.,* St. 23:6).

"This espousal we are dealing with is that which God makes known through Ezechiel by saying to the soul: 'And

171

passing by I looked at you and saw that it was the time for love, and I held My mantle over you and covered your nakedness [the soul is stripped of its imperfections as Jesus was stripped for His offering on the Cross]; I bound Myself by oath, I made a covenant with you . . . [the Bible explains that "hesed" is more than a contract but takes on the significance of married love, the warm, tender love that God has for the soul]. And you became mine. . . . I washed you with water . . . anointed you with oil . . . I put a beautiful crown upon your head. And you were adorned with gold and silver and clothed with fine linen and embroidered silk and many colors. . . . You grew more and more beautiful; and you rose to be queen. The fame of your beauty spread through the nations, since it was perfect, BECAUSE I HAD CLOTHED YOU WITH MY OWN SPLENDOR' (Ezekiel 16:5-14). . . . And so it happens with the soul of which we are speaking" (Ibid., St. 23:6).

The mystical experience of divine presence in creation is often depicted by the loving souls in the Old Testament. "Who, from the good things that are seen, have not been able to discover Him-Who-is, since through the grandeur and beauty of the creatures we may, by analogy, contemplate their Author" (Wisdom 13:1, 5).

"See the rainbow and praise its Maker" (Sirach 43:11).

John expresses his mystical awareness of God's presence in two of the best-loved stanzas of the *Spiritual Canticle:*

> *"My Beloved is the mountains,*
> *And lonely wooded valleys,*
> *Strange islands,*
> *And resounding rivers,*
> *The whistling of love-stirring breezes,*
>
> *"The tranquil night*
> *At the time of the rising dawn,*
> *Silent music,*
> *Sounding solitude,*
> *The supper that refreshes, and deepens love"*
>> *(Ibid.,* St. 14-15).

John states that the outward manifestation of God's beauty in creation is experienced interiorly by the bride/soul.

"It will happen that the soul will behold in herself the mountain of flowers mentioned above, which are the abundance, grandeur, and beauty of God; and intertwined among them, the lilies of the wooded valleys, which stand for rest, refreshment, and protection; and next, interspersed there, the fragrant roses of the strange islands, which we said was the strange knowledge of God. Then too she will be struck by the scent of the lilies beside the resounding rivers, which we said represented the greatness of God filling EVERY soul. And she will perceive from the jasmine interwoven there a fragrance diffused by the whistling of love-stirring breezes, which we also said the soul enjoys in this state. Likewise she is aware of all the other virtues and gifts we mentioned: the tranquil knowledge, silent music, sounding solitude, and the delightful and loving supper" *(Ibid.,* St. 24:6).

The flowers are the virtues and the breeze is the Holy Spirit, Who diffuses their fragrance. "Happy is the soul who in this life merits at some time the enjoyment of the fragrance of these divine flowers!" *(Ibid.,* St. 24:6).

"She lived in solitude,
And now in solitude has built her nest;
And in solitude He guides her,
He alone, Who also bears in solitude the wound of love"
(Ibid., St. 35:1).

John explains that God not only guided the soul "in her solitude, but that it is He alone Who works in her, without any means. This is a characteristic of the union of the soul with God in spiritual marriage: God works in and communicates Himself to her through Himself alone, without the intermediary of angels or natural ability, for the exterior and interior senses, and all creatures, and even the very soul do very little toward the reception of the remarkable supernatural favors which God grants in this state. They do not fall within the province of the soul's natural ability, or work, or diligence, but God alone grants them to her. . . . He is taken with love for her and wants to be the only one to grant her these favors. . . . That is, He is wounded with love for the bride" *(Ibid.,* St. 35:6-7).

For the bride/soul the beginning of the Beatific Vision can be experienced on earth. "In heaven we ourselves shall contemplate God, but, as it were, through the eyes of Christ. If this is so then our individual mystical effort awaits an essential completion in its union with the mystical effort of all other men [and women]. The divine milieu which will ultimately be one in the Pleroma, MUST BEGIN TO BECOME ONE DURING THE EARTHLY PHASE OF OUR EXISTENCE" *(The Divine Milieu,* Teilhard de Chardin, p. 143).

The Beatific Vision will not consist solely of gazing "at" God and basking in the rays for our own enjoyment, but "gazing with," having the divine viewpoint even on earth through "putting on the mind of Christ." The Gospel accounts of the life of Christ will become alive, for they are now the story of a dearly loved, personal Friend. Through the God-vision hidden treasures will be discovered in their depths. "I still have many things to say to you but they would be too much for you now. But when the Spirit of Truth comes He will lead you to complete truth" (John 16:12).

Since the beginning of time the hunger and thirst of the spirit have been leading souls to God. God has guided them through "a cloud by day [faith] and a fiery glow at night [love]" and through His messengers. The prophets often seemed to feel inadequate for the assignment and were reluctant to speak: "Do not say, 'I am a child.' . . . I am putting My words into your mouth" (Jeremiah 1:7, 9).

"Go and shout this in the hearing of Jerusalem: 'Yahweh says this; I remember the affection of your youth, the love of your bridal days: you followed me through the wilderness, through a land unsown' " (Jeremiah 2:1).

"They have abandoned Me, the fountain of living water, only to dig cisterns for themselves, leaky cisterns that hold no water" (Jeremiah 2:13).

But God does not accept this state as final, and pursues the soul like *The Hound of Heaven* (Francis Thompson), preparing the way with loving promises.

"You shall be My people and I will be your God. . . . They have found pardon in the wilderness. . . . I have loved you with an everlasting love, so I am constant in my affection for you. . . . I will comfort them as I lead them back; I will guide them to streams of water, by a smooth path where they will not stumble. . . . Their soul will be like a watered garden, they will sorrow no more" (Jeremiah 30:22; 31:2-3, 9, 12).

"Call to Me and I will answer you; I will tell you great mysteries of which you know nothing" (Jeremiah 33:3).

"I mean to spread peace everywhere" (Zechariah 8:12).

In preparation for His marriage of earth and heaven, God promises to purify souls, to "refine them as silver is refined, test them as gold is tested. They will call on My name and I shall listen: and I shall say: 'These are My people'; and each will say, 'Yahweh is my God!' . . . your God will come, and all the holy ones with Him. When that day comes, there will be no more cold, no more frost. It will be a day of wonder . . . running waters will issue from Jerusalem [the spiritual kingdom]" (Zechariah 13:9; 14:5).

There will be no separation of "sacred" and "worldly" when souls have the God-vision. "The horse bells will be inscribed with the words, 'Sacred to Yahweh' . . . every cooking pot . . . shall become sacred" (Zechariah 14:21).

Those who are sincerely trying to discern God's will need not worry. "I will make allowances for them as a man makes allowances for the son who obeys him. . . . The Sun of Righteousness will shine out with healing in its rays, You will leap like calves going out to pasture" (Malachi 1:17, 21).

"The kingdom of the world has become the kingdom of our Lord and His Christ, and He will reign for ever and ever" (Revelation 11:16).

For contemplative souls through the ages it was difficult to chronologically explain the glimpses of the "eternal now" experienced in their union with God beyond time. These were holistic experiences and could not be sorted out nor arranged in sequence. The similarity of that-which-was-experienced-as-a-whole is often discerned, although thousands of years may have separated the individuals who attempted to express the inexpressible. They were described according to the available knowledge of each individual's lifetime. But the message of God repeatedly comes through loud and clear. The world/soul is on a connecting course with the Divine. The Father, seeing us in the distance of time, hastens to meet us with "a ring and robe" at the first sign of response, to clothe us in His splendor, as He did the bride/soul. The world/soul's completion depends upon individual response. "Those who were ready went in with Him to the wedding hall. . . . So stay awake, because you do not know either the day or the hour" (Matthew 25:10).

The bride/soul who has been clothed with God's splendor has the necessary "wedding garments" which are a prerequisite for the eternal wedding feast. "The wedding is ready . . . invite everyone you can find to the wedding. So these servants went out on to the roads and collected together everyone they could find, bad and good alike: and the wedding hall was filled with guests. When the king came in to look at the guests he noticed one man who was not wearing a wedding garment, and said to him, 'How did you get in here, my friend, without a wedding garment?' And the man was silent. Then the king said to the attendants, 'Bind him hand and foot and throw him out into the dark, where there will be weeping and grinding of teeth' " (Matthew 22:8).

This spiritual evolution of the world is rooted in humanity's past, blooms in the present, and stretches into the future for, although "the Day of the Lord will come like a thief," "You must never forget that with the Lord, 'a day' can mean a thousand years and a thousand years is like a day. The Lord is not being slow to carry out His promises. . . . BUT HE IS BEING PATIENT WITH YOU ALL, WANTING NOBODY TO BE LOST . . . WHAT WE ARE WAITING FOR IS WHAT HE PROMISED: THE NEW HEAVENS AND NEW EARTH, the place where righteousness will be at home" (2 Peter 3:8, 10, 13).

"When the Son of Man comes, will He find any faith on earth?" (Luke 18:8).

"If you in your turn had only understood on this day the message of peace! . . . you did not recognize your opportunity when God offered it!" (Luke 19:42).

"You know how to read the face of the sky, but you cannot read the signs of the times" (Matthew 16:3).

"The only subject ultimately capable of mystical transfiguration is the whole group of mankind forming a single body and a single soul in charity" *(The Divine Milieu,* Teilhard de Chardin, p. 144).

In the *Spiritual Canticle,* John of the Cross also relates the individual soul's transformation to that of the developing world/soul or mystical body. He first states that the aim of the soul is a "love equal to God's" *(Spiritual Canticle,* St. 38:3) and that many divine gifts are included in "one essential glory" *(Ibid.,* St. 38:1).

"There You will show me what my soul has been seeking, and then You will give me, You, my Life, will give me there what You gave me on that other day" *(Ibid.,* St. 38:1). "By 'that other day,' she means the day of God's eternity, which is different from this temporal day. The 'what' is in point of fact the vision of God, but that which the vision of God is to the soul has no other name than 'what' " *(Ibid.,* St. 38:6).

"Yet in order to say something about it, let us repeat what Christ said of it to St. John seven times in the Apocalypse. . . . 'To him that overcomes I will give to eat of the tree of life which is in the paradise of my God' . . . 'Be faithful unto death and I will give you the crown of life.' Because this expression is inadequate also, He uses another which more obscure, yet explains it better: 'To him that overcomes I will give the hidden manna and a white stone, and on the stone a new name will be written which no one knows save he who receives it' (Revelation 2:17)" *(Spiritual Canticle,* St. 38:7).

"And because this is also an insufficient expression of

the 'what,' the Son of God uses another indicating great happiness and power. . . . 'And I will give him the morning star' (Revelation 2:28). . . . He then states: 'He that overcomes will thus be clothed in white garments, and I will not cross his name from the book of life. And I will confess his name before My Father' (Revelation 3:5)'' *(Ibid.,* St. 38:7).

"He then employs many terms to explain the 'what,' and they include in themselves unspeakable majesty and grandeur: 'And I will make him who overcomes a pillar in the temple of My God, and he shall go out no more. And I will write upon him the name of My God and the name of the city of My God, the new Jerusalem which comes down out of heaven from My God, and also My new name' (Revelation 3:12)'' *(Ibid.,* St. 38:8).

"And then He makes use of the seventh expression to explain the 'what': 'To him that overcomes I will give to sit with Me on My throne, as I also have conquered and sat with My Father on His throne. He who has ears to hear, let him hear' (Revelation 3:21-22)'' *(Ibid.,* St. 38:8).

"These are the words of the Son of God, explaining the 'what.' They cast the 'what' in very perfect terms, but they still do not explain it. This is a peculiarity of a thing that is immense: All the expressions of excellence, grandeur, and goodness are fitting, but do not explain it, not even when taken together'' *(Ibid.,* St. 38:8). "Consequently, a suitable expression for the 'what' of which the soul here speaks (the happiness toward which God predestined her) is undiscoverable'' *(Ibid.,* St. 38:9).

"Let us set aside this term 'what' which the soul uses and explain the verse in this way: What You gave me (that weight of glory to which You predestined me, O my Spouse, on the day of Your eternity when You considered it good to decree my creation), You will give me then on the day of my espousals and nuptials and on my day of gladness of heart, when loosed from the flesh and within the high caverns of Your chamber, gloriously transformed in You, I shall drink with You the juice of the sweet pomegranates" (*Ibid.*, St. 38:9).

"The pomegranates stand for the mysteries of Christ. . . . Just as pomegranates have many little seeds, formed and sustained within the circular shell, so each of the attributes, mysteries, judgments, and virtues of God, like a round shell of power and mystery, holds and sustains a multitude of marvelous decrees and wondrous effects. Let us remark here the circular or spherical figure of the pomegranate, for each pomegranate symbolizes some divine attribute and power, and each divine attribute and power is God Himself, Who is represented by the circular or spherical figure because He has no beginning or end" (*Ibid.*, St. 37:7).

"O souls, created for these grandeurs and called to them! What are you doing? How are you spending your time?" (*Ibid.*, St. 39:7).

Epilogue

"Parer — Latin parare, to prepare, to make ready, adorn."

"Parere — To appear, come forth."

"Parous — Latin parere, to bear, beget, a combining form used to signify giving birth to, bearing, producing."

"PAROUSIA — Greek, lit. presence, to be present, advent, in Graeco-Roman world was used for official visits by royalty, arrival of a royal presence."

The world, individually and collectively, is called to participate in preparations for a spiritual birth, the arrival of a Royal Presence — Parousia. The "world-soul," or "mystical body," is made up of a mosaic of individual souls, each reflecting a unique Divine Image. A kaleidoscope of souls is needed to more adequately reflect the Divine Immensity. The "world-soul" could be compared to the multi-faceted mirrored globe that revolves at parties and dances, and reflects all the colors of the rainbow from a single light source. Since two contraries cannot co-exist, as each mirror-soul reflects the divine light to the fullness of its capacity, the "darkness" will eventually be eliminated.

"It will never be night again and they will not need lamplight or sunlight, because the Lord God will be shining on them. They will reign for ever and ever. The angel said to me, 'All that you have written is sure and will come true' " (Revelation 22:5-6).

The final battle is between the forces of good and evil. It is first of all an interior conflict which must be gradually resolved in each soul, since each soul is part of the New Jerusalem. Through its contemplative relationship the soul is not only in union with God and discerning His will, but through the "communion of Saints" is united with all of those souls who have been brought to divine transformation, for they are one in God. They have achieved their birth into eternal life and are now participating in the divine nature, loving with God's own powerful, all-embracing love. They are concerned for us as younger brothers and sisters, for they love with the same love as the Father, Son, and Holy Spirit. As we learn to allow God's love (agape) and will to surface more and more within us, we are tapping this power, drawing on this energy. The growing love of billions of souls on earth, joining with the perfect love of countless souls transformed in God, is an unconquerable force. God is Love, and Love conquers all.

"The Kingdom of God is not just words, it is power" (1 Corinthians 3:21).

"Be brave; I have conquered the world" (John 16:33).

Many people in our world are troubled about the possibility of a nuclear holocaust. "When you hear of wars and rumours of wars, do not be alarmed, this is something that must happen, but the end will not be yet. For nation will fight against nation, and kingdom against kingdom. There will be earthquakes here and there; there will be famines. This is the beginning of the birthpangs" (Mark 13:7).

"He has let us know the mystery of His purpose, the hidden plan He so kindly made in Christ from the beginning to act upon when the times had run their course to the end: that He would bring everything together under Christ, as head, everything in the heavens and everything on earth" (Ephesians 1:9).

"From the beginning till now the entire creation, as we know, has been groaning in one great act of giving birth"

(Romans 8:22).

Being part of creation, everyone is directly involved in spiritual rebirth. All people, whether male or female, have the intrinsic capacity for "spiritual maternity." Each person has an ever-developing divine life within, the Christ-in-us which is destined to be born into eternal life. Mary, the Living Tabernacle, is our prototype. Male or female, we are all spiritual Marys, nurturing and encouraging the growth of divine life within us, and bringing it not only to eternal birth, but to many spiritual "births" here and now in the world, cooperating with Divine Love to be spiritually "fruitful and multiply and fill the earth."

"A man suffers all these afflictive purgations of spirit that he may be reborn in the life of the spirit by means of this divine inflow, and through these sufferings the spirit of salvation is brought forth in fulfillment of the words of Isaias: 'In Your presence, O Lord, we have conceived and been in the pains of labor and have brought forth the spirit of salvation' " (The Dark Night, St. John of the Cross, Bk. II, ch. 9:6).

The wounded world has endured many "dark nights" but the glimmer of dawn is at last approaching. It is a joyful time, a spiritual spring, a time to rejoice. "A voice cries 'Prepare in the wilderness a way for Yahweh. Make a straight highway for our God across the desert . . . then the glory of Yahweh shall be revealed and ALL MANKIND shall see [experience] it" (Isaiah 40:3, 5).

At the opening of Vatican II, Pope John XXIII declared "A new Pentecost." Other observers call it "spiritual evolution" but, whatever the designation, God's increasing activity through the Holy Spirit cannot be ignored. "I will pour out My Spirit on all mankind" (Joel 3:28). Everywhere there is a spiritual awakening, a new dynamism, gifts of healing, charismatics and other prayer groups, and a renewed interest in Scripture studies. There seems to be a spiritual resurrection, an awakening of the "sleeping giant" — the laity — meant to collaborate with God in

183

transforming the world.

"He overpowered the dragon, that primeval serpent which is the devil and Satan, and chained him up for a thousand years. . . . They came to life, and reigned with Christ for a thousand years. This is the FIRST RESURREC-TION. . . . Happy and blessed are those who share in the first resurrection; the second death [of the body] cannot affect them but they will be priests of God and of Christ and reign with Him for a thousand years" (Revelation 20:2, 5-6).

"You are a chosen race, a royal priesthood, a consecrated nation, a people set apart to sing the praises of God Who called you out of the darkness into His wonderful light. Once you were not a people at all and now you are the People of God" (1 Peter 2:9).

This "spiritual priesthood" ordained by God is a sharing in the healing and consecration of the world. True healing and consecrating begins interiorly, from our depths. The world of science knows that to change an element, you must change its nucleus. Since we are all a part of the world's woundedness, we are all a part of the world's restoration. From the beginning of time we have been receiving the same message from God through His various Prophets, Apostles, Saints, and holy people.

"You did not see Him, yet you love Him; and still without seeing Him, you are already filled with a JOY so glorious that it cannot be described, because you believe; AND YOU ARE SURE OF THE END TO WHICH YOUR FAITH LOOKS FORWARD, that is, the salvation of your souls. It was this salvation that the prophets were looking and searching so hard for; their prophecies were about the grace which was to come to you. THE SPIRIT OF CHRIST WHICH WAS IN THEM foretold the sufferings of Christ and the glories that would come after them, and they tried to find out at what time and in what circumstances all this was to be expected. It was revealed to them that the news they brought of all the things which have now been announced to you, by those who preached to you the Good News through the Holy Spirit sent from heaven, was FOR YOU and not for themselves" (1 Peter 1:8-12).

"The Spirit you received is not the spirit of slaves bringing fear into your lives again; it is the spirit of sons [and daughters], and it makes us cry out, 'Abba, Father!' The Spirit Himself and our spirit bear united witness that we are children of God" (Romans 8:14).

God does not desire the destruction of the world, but longs to heal and restore it, then unite His children to Himself. In this He expects their cooperation and participation as "laborers in the vineyards" or "good stewards."

"He wants EVERYONE to be saved and reach full knowledge of the truth" (1 Timothy 2:4).

"For now I create new heavens and a new earth, and the past will not be remembered, and will come no more to men's minds. Be glad and rejoice forever and ever for what I am creating, because I now create Jerusalem 'Joy' and her people 'Gladness.' I shall rejoice over Jerusalem and exult in my people" (Isaiah 65:17).

"Rejoice, Jerusalem. . . . Now towards her I send flowing peace, like a river. . . . At the sight your heart will rejoice. . . . To His servants Yahweh will reveal His hand. . . . For see how Yahweh comes in fire. . . . I am coming to gather the nations of every language. They shall come to witness My glory. . . . All mankind will come to bow down in My presence, says Yahweh" (Isaiah 66:12, 18, 24).

"What we are waiting for is what He promised: the new heavens and new earth, the place where righteousness will be at home" (2 Peter 3:13).

"Live in Christ, then, my children, so that if He appears, we may have full confidence, and not turn from Him in shame at His coming" (1 John 2:28).

"It is He Who is coming on the clouds: EVERYONE will see [EXPERIENCE] Him" (Revelation 1:7).

"The only human embrace capable of worthily enfolding the divine is that of all men [and women] opening their arms to call down and welcome the fire. The only subject ultimately capable of mystical transfiguration is the whole group of mankind forming a single body and a single soul in charity" (*The Divine Milieu,* Teilhard de Chardin, p. 144).

The human race is rounding a spiritual "time curve" and moving into a new era. In past centuries many people who felt drawn to a life of deeper intimacy with God would seek spiritual growth through a "religious vocation." By withdrawing from temporal matters they desired to give their undivided love and attention to the divine and, through prayer and study, would become familiar through experience with the various stages of the soul's spiritual journey.

In this "new beginning" God is not waiting for His children to turn to Him, but is actively seeking them, "surfacing," so to speak, from the deepest center of countless human lives. For those unfamiliar with the process by which the spirit develops during our earthly existence, or unaware of their divine inheritance, it could be a mystifying and confusing experience.

To consider the Divine only as outside and beyond our human condition, and God as far removed from our insignificant lives, is to render ineffectual our greatest source of hope. In addition, many people try to appropriate more guilt than they are actually entitled to. This type of mindset tends to block the inflow of God's forgiving, transforming love, which is as necessary to our spiritual wholeness as human love is to the sound psychological development of infants and children. For these persons the positive, loving and forgiving aspects of God's Self-revelation need to be re-examined and emphasized.

"They will all know Me, the least no less than the greatest — it is Yahweh Who speaks — since I will forgive their iniquity and never call their sin to mind. . . . They have found pardon in the wilderness. . . . I have loved you with an everlasting love, so I am constant in My affection for you" (Jeremiah 31:2-3, 34).

"How often have I longed to gather your children, as a hen gathers her chicks under her wings" (Matthew 23:37).

In contemplative prayer souls return to their beginnings, finding them fresh and new in the heightened awareness of contemplative vision. From our Judaeo-Christian roots through the first fifteen centuries of Christianity, contemplation has been essential to the spiritual health and vitality of all people. It is time for the living waters of contemplation to be re-channeled into the mainstream of Christianity.

"The Lamb Who is at the throne will be their Shepherd and will lead them to springs of living water; and God will wipe away all tears from their eyes" (Revelation 7:17).

Although the Persons of the Trinity are All in all, the Age of Creation is generally attributed to God the Father, the Era of Redemption to God the Son, and the emerging Age of Sanctification to the Holy Spirit. We who are living in this Age of the Spirit are chosen to "make ready the way of the Lord," along the spiritual pathway of our souls.

"When that day comes, word will come to Jerusalem: Zion, have no fear, do not let your hands fall limp. Yahweh your God is in your midst, a victorious warrior. He will exult with joy over you, He will renew you by His love; He will dance with shouts of joy for you as on a day of festival" (Zephaniah 3:17).

"In the tender compassion of our God the dawn from on high shall break upon us, to shine on those who dwell in darkness and the shadow of death, and to guide our feet into the way of peace" (Luke 1:68).

External change is more popular than interior change, but God's peace, which is the only permanent and lasting peace, develops from the inside out. What the world considers peace is no more than a lull between wars.

"The Advocate, the Holy Spirit, Whom the Father will send in My name, will teach you everything and remind you of all I have said to you. Peace I bequeath to you, MY

OWN PEACE I GIVE YOU, A PEACE THE WORLD CAN-
NOT GIVE, this is My gift to you. Do not let your hearts be
troubled or afraid" (John 14:26).

The prayerful soul, united with God, radiates His healing attributes, divine love, joy, and peace into a wounded
world. The light of our inner peace is each soul's contribu-
tion to the final transformation of the world.

"You will have in you the strength, based on His own
glorious power, never to give in, but to bear anything
joyfully, thanking the Father Who has made it possible for
you to join the saints and with them to INHERIT THE
LIGHT" (Colossians 1:11).

"Very soon now, I shall be with you again. . . . I, Jesus,
have sent My angel to make these revelations to you for the
sake of the churches. I am of David's line, the root of
David and the Bright Star of the Morning. The Spirit and
the Bride say, 'Come.' Let everyone who listens answer,
'Come.' Then let all who are thirsty come: all who want it
may have the water of life, and have it free" (Revelation
22:12, 16).

References

The Collected Works of St. Teresa of Avila, Volume One.
   The Book of Her Life
   Spiritual Testimonies
   Soliloquies

The Collected Works of St. Teresa of Avila, Volume Two
   The Way of Perfection
   Meditations on the Song of Songs
   The Interior Castle

The Collected Works of St. John of the Cross
   The Ascent of Mount Carmel
   The Dark Night
   The Spiritual Canticle
   The Living Flame of Love

Drawing on the Right Side of the Brain, Betty Edwards, copyright © 1979, published by J.P. Tarcher, Inc., 9110 Sunset Blvd., Los Angeles, California 90069.

Most biblical quotations are from the Jerusalem Bible.

Offices of the Secular Order
of the Discalced Carmelites in the United States

Eastern States Jurisdiction (Washington, D.C., Province)
Central Office of the Secular Order, 1233 South 45th St., Milwaukee, Wisconsin 53214.

Central States Jurisdiction (Oklahoma Province)
Central Office of the Secular Order, Route 4, Box 1150, Little Rock, Arkansas 72206.

Western States Jurisdiction (California-Arizona Delegation)
Central Office of the Secular Order, P.O. Box 3079/12455 Clayton Road, San Jose, California 95127.